NARRATIVE

OF A

VOYAGE TO SENEGAL

IN 1816.

No person can read this Interesting Narrative without being deeply affected by the perils and misfortunes to which the small remnant of persons, who were saved from this deplorable Shipwreck, were exposed. Of one hundred and fifty persons embarked upon the raft, and left to their fate, only fifteen remained alive thirteen days afterwards; but of these fifteen, so miraculously saved, life constituted the sole possession, being literally stripped of every thing. At Paris, some benevolent individuals have recently opened a subscription for their relief. Should any persons, in this country, feel disposed to contribute to this humane object, Mr. Colburn will feel great pleasure in becoming the medium for transmitting their subscriptions to the unfortunate sufferers.

KING ZAIDE,

Drawn at the moment when this Prince desired M. Kummer to relate the History of the last French Revolution!

Published by Henry Colburn, Conduit Street, April 1 1818

NARRATIVE

OF A

VOYAGE TO SENEGAL

IN 1816;

UNDERTAKEN BY ORDER OF THE FRENCH GOVERNMENT,

COMPRISING AN ACCOUNT

OF THE

Shipwreck of the Medusa,

THE SUFFERINGS OF THE CREW,

AND THE VARIOUS OCCURRENCES ON BOARD THE RAFT,

IN THE DESERT OF ZAARA, AT ST. LOUIS,

AND AT THE CAMP OF DACCARD.

TO WHICH ARE SUBJOINED

OBSERVATIONS RESPECTING THE AGRICULTURE

OF THE

WESTERN COAST OF AFRICA,

FROM CAPE BLANCO TO THE MOUTH OF THE GAMBIA.

BY

J. B. HENRY SAVIGNY,

AND

ALEXANDER CORRÉARD.

ILLUSTRATED WITH THE NOTES OF M. BREDIF,
AND EMBELLISHED WITH
A PLAN OF THE RAFT, AND A PORTRAIT OF KING ZAIDE.

LONDON:

PRINTED FOR HENRY COLBURN, CONDUIT-STREET.

1818.

ADVERTISEMENT.

At the moment that we publish a Second Edition of our Narrative, we learn that Mr. Sevigny* is going to publish a pretended Ac-

---

* This Mr. Sevigny must not be confounded with Mr. Savigny, one of the authors of this narrative.

This Mr. Sevigny is one of the directors of an anonymous company, which one of the King's Ministers has recommended in the following manner:

"The keeper of the seals has informed the magis-
"trates, that an anonymous company, which had formed
"itself under the name of the *Colonial Philanthropic*
"*Society of Senegambia*, and which announced the pro-
"ject of procuring for all those who should confide in
"it, colonial establishments on the coasts near Cape Verd,
"has received no authority from the government, and
"that, on the steps which it has taken, to obtain such
"authority, it has been found that it was not in a condi-
"tion to fulfil its promises, which, therefore, were a kind
"of snare, for those whom they might have seduced. It
"has been, consequently, prohibited from making any
"enterprise, or any expedition. The agents of this Society
"having no other object than to deceive the public
"credulity, must be denounced to his Majesty's Attorney-
"General, who will take against them the measures pre-
"scribed by the law."

(*Journal des Débats, Novembre* 24, 1817.)

count, by Mr. Richefort, an auxiliary Ex-Officer of the French Marine.

Our readers will not have forgotten a certain pretended sea-officer who was partly the cause of our misfortunes, and who, when on board the Medusa, gave such unhappy advice to the captain, who still more unhappily, followed it too closely; well; this *ex-officer*, this fatal *auxiliary*, who conducted the frigate upon the bank of Arguin, is no other than Mr. Richefort!

Having gone on board the governor's boat, he remained a stranger to the disasters which he had partly caused, and consequently, knew nothing of what passed, either upon the raft, or on board the boats which stranded, or in the desert.

We make no farther remarks; the public will judge of his account and ours.

CORRÉARD AND SAVIGNY.

PREFACE.

The annals of the marine, record no example of a shipwreck so terrible as that of the Medusa frigate. Two of the unfortunate crew, who have miraculously escaped from the catastrophe, impose upon themselves the painful and delicate task, of describing all the circumstances which attended it.

It was in the midst of the most cruel sufferings that we took the solemn resolution, to make known, to the civilized world, all the details of our unhappy adventure, if heaven permitted us again to see our dear country. We should believe that we failed in our duty to ourselves, and to our fellow citizens, if we left buried in oblivion facts which the public must be desirous to know. All the details of the events at which we were not present, have been communicated to us by respectable persons, who have warranted their authenticity. We shall, besides, advance nothing which cannot be proved.

Here, we hear some voices ask, what right we have to make known to the government, men who are, perhaps, guilty, but whom their places, and their rank, entitle to more respect. They are ready to make it a crime in us, that we have dared to say, that officers of the marine had abandoned us. But what interest, we ask, in our turn, should cause a fatal indulgence to be claimed for those, who have failed in their duties; while the destruction of a hundred and fifty wretches, left to the most cruel fate, scarcely excited a murmur of disapprobation? Are we still in those times, when men and things were sacrificed to the caprices of favour? Are the resources and the dignities of the State, still the exclusive patrimony of a privileged class? and are there other titles to places and honours, besides merit and talents?

Let us venture to advance another truth, a truth useful to the Minister himself. There exists among the officers of the Marine, an intractable *esprit de corps*, a pretended point of honour, equally false and arrogant, which leads them to consider as an insult to the whole navy, the discovery of one guilty individual. This inadmissible principle, which is useful only to insignificance, to intrigue, to people the least worthy to call on the name of honour, has the most ruinous consequences for the State, and the public service. By this, incapacity and baseness are always covered with a guilty veil, which they dare to attempt to render sacred; by this, the favours of government are bestowed at random, upon persons, who impose upon it the strange obligation of being perpetually in the dark respecting them. Under the protection of this obligation of officious silence, hitherto seconded by the slavery of the press, men without talents survive every revolution, exhibit in every antichamber their privileged incapacity, and braving public opinion, even that of their comrades, who are the first victims of a foolish and arrogant prejudice, which deceives them, shew themselves more eager to monopolise favours and honours, in proportion as they are less able to render themselves worthy of them.

We shall believe that we have deserved well of our government, if our faithful narrative can make it sensible how much its confidence is abused. Just, besides, and not animated by passion, it is with real pleasure that we shall make those known, who, by their conduct in our shipwreck, have acquired a right to general esteem. Others will doubtless complain of the severity of our accusing language; but honest men will grant us their approbation. If we hear it said, that our frankness may have been useful to our country, this success will be, at once, our justification and our recompence.

We have questioned, concerning the nautical details, several gentlemen of the navy who were on board; we confess, however, that on comparing their accounts, we have observed that they did not always entirely agree; but we have taken those facts which had the most witnesses in their favour. We shall be sometimes obliged to record cruel truths; they will, however, be directed only to those, whose unskilfulness, or pusillanimity have caused these dreadful events. We venture to affirm, that the numerous observations, which we have collected, will give to our work all the accuracy rigorously required in so interesting a narrative.

We must observe to our readers that it has been impossible for us to avoid the use of naval terms, which will, perhaps, give a great degree of roughness to our narrative, but we hope that the public who are always indulgent, will be so on this occasion, to two unfortunate men, who pretend only to make them acquainted with the truth, and not to give them a superior work. Besides, as we in a manner, submit these events, to the judgment of the gentlemen of the French Navy, it was necessary to make use of the technical terms, that they might be able to understand us.

This second edition is enriched with notes, which will give the reader interesting details on many points, which in the former we could only slightly touch upon. He will have nothing more to desire, particularly respecting the march in the desert after the stranding of the long-boat.

These notes begin with the moment that the frigate stranded, and terminate with the arrival at St. Louis.

They were communicated to us by Mr. Landry, an officer of the Royal University, Professor

Emeritus of the Academy of Paris, and at present at the head of a school or Academy, in the Rue Cerisaye, No. 2, quarter of the Arsenal, at Paris. He has had the kindness to extract them for us from a narrative, written by his nephew, Mr. Bredif, Engineer of Mines, belonging to the expedition to Senegal.

The Narrator sent this account to his family above a year ago, addressing it to his sister The reader will, therefore, not be surprised at the tone of simplicity which prevails in this recital. Mr. Landry would not take away any part for fear of injuring the truth of the circumstances, by meddling with it. If Mr. Bredif, is always placed in the fore-ground, that is not surprising; in a sister, a brother is the principal object which she cannot lose sight of for a moment.

He who loves to observe men, in all the circumstances, in which they may be placed, will easily judge, after what Mr. Bredif did or felt, what may have been done or felt by the sharers in the same misfortunes, who are, besides, never forgotten.

Mr. Bredif is now in the interior of Africa, employed upon the Mission which the government has entrusted to him; the last accounts from him are of the 14th of October, 1817. The manner in which he knows how to give an account of the facts which he has observed, and still more the courage, the prudence, and humanity, which he displayed in the disaster of the Medusa, and in all that followed it, give reason to hope, and this hope cannot be deceived, that he will duly execute his Mission, and render himself worthy of his Majesty's favours.

PLAN of the RAFT of the MEDUSA,
at the moment of its being abandoned

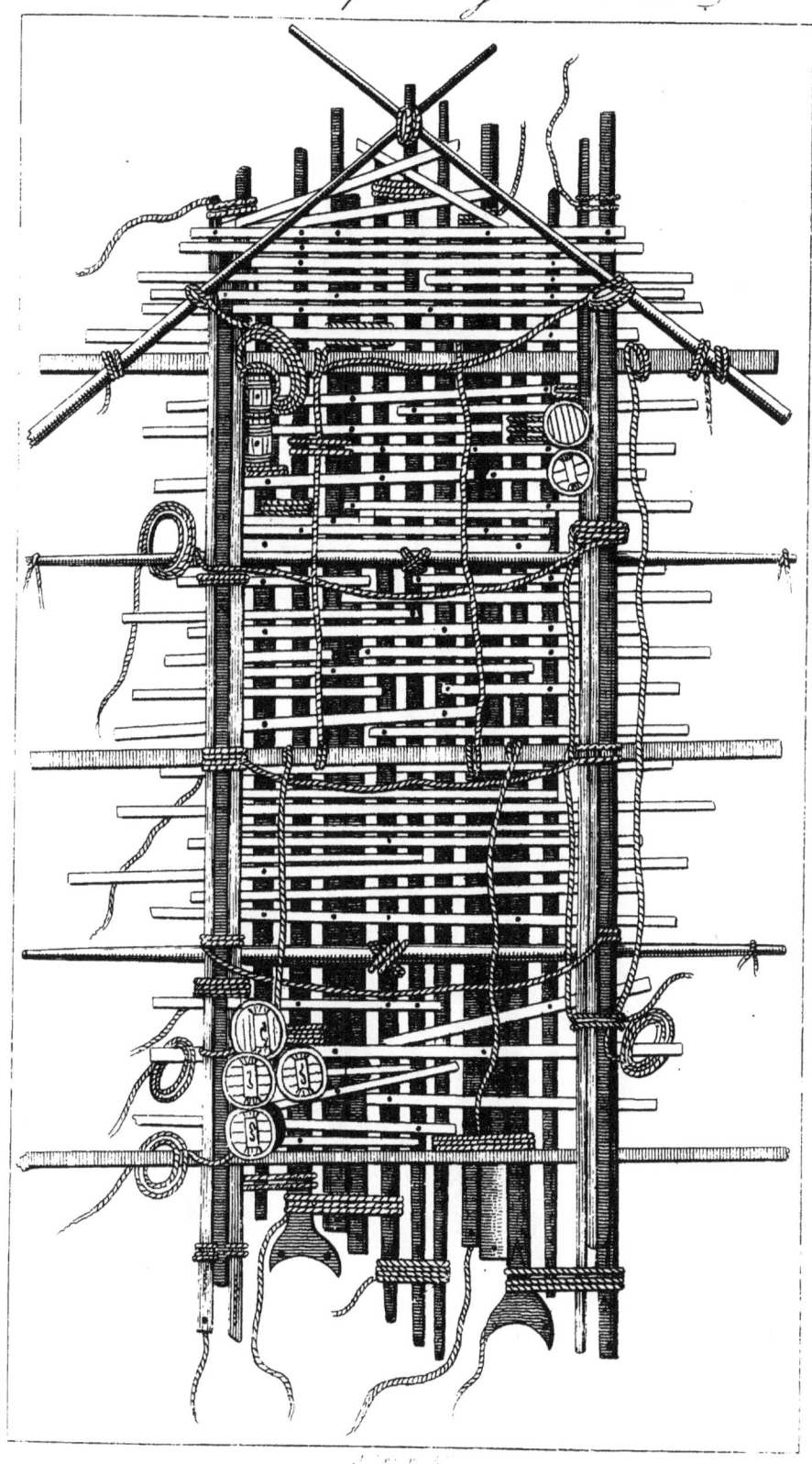

150 Frenchmen were placed on this Machine 15 only were saved 13 days after

NARRATIVE

OF

A VOYAGE TO SENEGAL.

INTRODUCTION.

THE French settlements, situated on the western coast of Africa, from Cape Blanco to the mouth of the river Gambia, have been alternately possessed by France and England, and have remained definitively in the hands of the French, whose ancestors laid the foundations of them previously to the fourteenth century, when they discovered this country.

The English made themselves masters in 1758 of the Isle of St. Louis, the seat of the general government of all the settlements which the French have on that part of the coast: we recovered it twenty years after, in 1779: and our possessions were again confirmed to us by the treaty of peace between France and England, concluded on the 3d of September, 1783. In 1808, our possessions fell again into the power of the English, less by the superiority of their arms, than by the treachery of some individuals unworthy of bearing the name of Frenchmen. They were finally restored to us by the treaties of peace of 1814, and 1815, which confirmed that of 1783 in its whole extent.

The stipulations of this treaty regulate the respective rights of the two nations on the Western coast of Africa; they fix the possessions of France as follows:— from Cape Blanco situated in longitude 19° 30′, and latitude 20° 55′ 30″, to the mouth of the river Gambia in longitude 19° 9′, and latitude 13°; they guarantee this property exclusively to our country, and only permit the English to trade together with the French, for gum, from the river St. John to Fort Portendick inclusive, on condition, that they shall not form establishments of any kind whatsoever in this river, or upon any point of this coast. Only it is said, that the possession of the factory of Albreda, situated at the mouth of the river Gambia, and that of fort James, are confirmed to England.

The rights of the two nations being thus regulated, France thought of resuming her possessions and the enjoyment of her rights. The minister of the marine after having long meditated, and taken two years to prepare an expedition of four vessels, at last gave orders that it should sail for Senegal. The following is a list of the persons who composed the expedition.

A Colonel, to command in chief for the king on the whole coast from Cape Blanco to the mouth of the river Gambia, and charged with the superior direction of the administration............... 1

A Lieutenant-Colonel, (chef de bataillon) commandant of Goree.... 1

A Lieutenant-Colonel commanding the African battalion, composed of three companies of 84 men each.. 253

A Lieutenant of Artillery, inspector of the powder magazines and batteries, and commanding ten workmen of his arm.................. 11

A Commissary, inspector of the marine, chief of the administration . 1
Four Store-keepers 4
Six Clerks 6
Four Scouts (guetteurs)......... 4
Two Curés................... 2
Two Schoolmasters (instituteurs) 2
Two Writers (greffiers, they supply the place of the notaries and even of the mayors)................. 2
Two Hospital Directors 2
Two Apothecaries...... 2
Five Surgeons............. ... 5
Two Port Captains 2
Three Pilots 3
A Gardener................. 1
Eighteen Women 18
Eight Children 8
Four Bakers 4

Farther for an intended expedition into the country of Galam.

An Engineer of mines 1
A Geographical Engineer...... 1
A Naturalist (cultivateur naturaliste) 1

Farther for an expedition which

was to seek upon Cape Verd, or in its neighbourhood for a spot proper for the foundation of a colony.

A Physician	1
An Agriculturist for European productions	1
An Agriculturist for colonial productions	1
Two Geographical Engineers	2
A Naturalist	1
An officer of the marine	1
Twenty workmen	20
Three Women	3
Total	365

This expedition consisted therefore of 365 persons, of whom about 240 were embarked on board the *Medusa* frigate.

NARRATIVE,

&c. &c.

On the 17th of June, 1816, at seven in the morning, the expedition for Senegal sailed from the roads of the Island of Aix, under the command of Captain Chaumareys; the vessels composing it were the *Medusa** frigate of 44 guns, Captain Chaumareys; the *Echo*† corvette, Captain Cornet de Venancourt; the flute *La Loire*, commanded by Lieutenant Giquel Destouches; and the *Argus*‡ brig, commanded by Lieutenant Parnajon. The wind was northerly, blowing a fresh breeze; we carried all our sails; but had hardly cleared the port when the

---

* The *Medusa* was armed en flute, having only 14 guns on board; it was equipped at Rochefort with the *Loire*.

† Equipped at Brest.

‡ Came from L'Orient.

wind scanted a little, and we tacked to double the Tower of Chassiron, which is placed at the extremity of the Isle of Oleron.* After having plied to windward the whole day, in the evening about five o'clock, the *Loire* being unable to stem the currents which were at that time contrary, and hindered her from entering the *passes*, desired leave to cast anchor; M. de Chaumareys granted it, and ordered the whole squadron to anchor. We were then half a league from the Isle of Rhé, within what is called the " *Pertuis d'Antioche.*" We cast anchor the first, and all the other vessels came and placed themselves near us. The *Loire* being a dull sailer, was the last which came to an anchor. The weather was fine: the wind N.W. and consequently too near to allow us to double Chassiron, with a contrary current. At seven in the evening, at the beginning of the ebb, we weighed anchor, and hoisted our sails; all the other vessels did the same: the signal to get under way had been

---

* The town of Chassiron is on the point of Oleron, opposite a bank of rocks called *Les Antiochats.*

given them a few minutes before. At night we found ourselves between the lights of Chassiron and La Baleine.* A few moments sufficed to double them; we were scarcely clear, when the wind became almost calm; the vessels no longer obeyed the helm, the sky grew dark, the sea was very hollow, in short every thing announced a storm; the wind threatened to blow from the west, and consequently to become contrary; it was variable and squally; towards ten o'clock it was perceived that we were running directly upon a danger, called *Les Roches Bonnes.*† We tacked to escape certain destruction; between eleven and twelve at night, a storm arose in the north, and brought on wind from that quarter; we were then able to advance; the clouds dispersed, and the next day the weather was very fine, with a breeze from the N. E. but very faint;

---

* The light house of La Baleine is placed at the other end of the Pertuis d'Antioche, on the coast of the Isle of Rhé.

† *Les Roches Bonnes* are 8 or 9 leagues from the Isle of Rhé, their position is not exactly determined on the charts.

for some days we made but very little progress.

On the 21st or 22d we doubled Cape Finisterre; beyond this point which bounds the Gulph of Gascony, the *Loire* and the *Argus* parted company; these vessels sailing very ill, it was impossible for them to keep up with the frigate, which to enable them to do so, would have been obliged to take in her top-gallant sails and studding sails.

The *Echo* alone was in sight, but at a great distance, and carrying a press of sail not to lose sight of us. The frigate was so much a better sailer than the corvette, that with a small quantity of sail, she not only kept up with her, but even got a-head of her in a surprising manner; the wind had freshened and we were going at the rate of nine knots. *

An unfortunate accident disturbed the pleasure we felt at being so favoured by the wind; a sailor lad 15 years of age, fell into the sea, through one of the fore port-holes,

---

* Three knots make a marine league of 5556 meters.

on the larboard side; a great many persons were at the time, on the poop and the breast work, looking at the gambols of the porpoises.* The exclamations of pleasure at beholding the sports of these animals, were succeeded by cries of pity; for some moments the unfortunate youth held by the end of a rope, which he caught hold of in his fall; but the rapidity with which the frigate sailed, soon forced him to let go; a signal was made to acquaint the *Echo* with this accident; that vessel was at a considerable distance, and we were going to fire a gun to second the signal, but there was not one loaded, however we threw out the life buoy.† The sails

---

* These are very large fish which every moment appear on the surface of the water, where they tumble about. They pass with such prodigious rapidity, that they will swim round a ship, when it is going at the rate of nine or ten knots an hour.

† The life buoy, is made of cask staves hooped together, and is about a metre (something more than a yard.) in diameter, in the middle of which is a little mast to fix a flag to. It is thrown into the sea, as soon as a man falls overboard, that he may place himself upon it while the operation of lowering a boat down, or heaving the vessel to, is performed.

were clewed up, and the ship hove to. This manœuvre was long; we should have come to the wind, as soon as they cried, " a man overboard," it is true that somebody cried aloud from the poop, that he was saved; and a sailor had indeed caught him by the arm, but he had been obliged to let him go, because he would have been pulled overboard himself: a boat was however let down; it was a six-oared barge in which there were only three men: it was all in vain; and after having looked for some time, the boat came on board again without having found even the buoy. If the unfortunate youth, who seemed to swim pretty well, had strength to reach it, he doubtless perished on it, after having experienced the most cruel sufferings. The ship was trimmed, and we resumed our course.

The *Echo* rejoined us, and for some time she kept within hail; but we soon lost her. On the 26th, we plied to windward during the night, fearing lest we should strike on the eight rocks, which are situated the most *Northerly*, in 34° 45′, Latitude, and the most *Southerly* in latitude, 34° 30', so that the extent of this danger is about five leagues from *North* to *South* and about four leagues from *East* to *West*: the most southerly rock is distant about forty leagues to the *North*, 5° East, from the East point of Madeira.

On the 27th, in the morning we expected to see the island of Madeira, we however proceeded to no purpose till noon, at which hour we made an observation to ascertain our situation. The solar observation made us East, and West of Porto Santo; we continued on the same tack, and in the evening at sunset, the man at the mast head discovered, land.* This error

---

* We do not know why the government makes its vessels take this route; when one can proceed directly to the Canaries: it is true they are often obscured by mists, but there are no dangers in the principal canals which they form, and they extend over so large a space that it is impossible not to recognise them, with facility. They have also the advantage of being placed in the course of the monsoons; though however, westwinds sometimes blow for several days together. We think that vessels going to the East Indies might dispense with making Madeira and Porto Santo, the more so as there are many shoals near

in the arrival, was at least thirty leagues in the East. It was attributed to the currents of the straits of Gibraltar; if this error really arises from the currents of the strait, it merits the attention of vessels which frequent these seas. The whole night we proceeded with few sails up; at midnight we tacked, in order not to approach too near to the land.

The next morning at day break we saw very distinctly the islands of Madeira and Porto Santo; on the larboard, were those called Desert; Madeira was at least twelve leagues off: sailing before the wind we made nine knots, and in a few hours we were very near it. For a considerable time we ran along the coast of the island at a small distance from shore: we passed before the principal towns, Funchal and Do Sob.

Madeira appears like an amphitheatre;

---

these islands; besides the rocks, of which we have spoken above there is another. to the N. E. of Porto Santo, on which many vessels have been lost; by night all these reefs are very dangerous, by day they are recognised by the breakers on them.

the country houses which cover it seem to be in a very good taste, and give it a charming appearance. All these delightful habitations are surrounded by fine gardens, and fields covered with orange and lemon trees, which when the wind blows from the shore, diffuse for full half a league in the open sea, the most agreeable perfume. The hills are covered with vineyards, bordered with banian trees: in short every thing is combined to render Madeira one of the most beautiful islands of Africa. Its soil is only a vegetable sand, mixed with an ash, which gives it astonishing fertility; it shews every where nothing but the remains of a volcanised earth, the colour of which is that of the element, by which it was long consumed. Funchal, the capital town of the islands is situated in long. 19°. 20″. 30.″ in lat. 32° 37′. 40′. This town is far from handsome, the streets are narrow, and the houses in general ill built: the highest part of the island is the Pic de Ruvio, which rises about two hundred metres above the level of the sea. The population of Madeira is from 85,000 to 90,000, inhabitants as we are assured by a person worthy of credit, who has resided for some time in that fine colony.

We sailed in this manner along the coast of Madeira, because the intention of the commander was to send a boat on shore for refreshments; but being surprised by a calm under the land, we were afraid of approaching too near, lest we should not be able to stem the strong currents which set towards it. A gentle breeze arising, enabled us to get out to sea, where the wind became favorable, and pretty brisk; it was resolved that the boat should not go on shore: and we resumed our course going at eight knots. We had remained three hours opposite Funchal bay. At nightfall Madeira was in full sight: the next morning at sun-rise we saw the islands called Salvages, and in the evening we descried the Pico of Teneriffe, on the island of that name. This lofty mountain, behind which the sun had just set, presented a sight truly magnificent; its summit seemed to be crowned with fire:

its elevation above the level of the sea, is 3711 metres; it is situated in lat. 28° 17′ and in long. 19°. Several persons on board affirmed that they saw the Pico at eight o'clock in the morning; and yet we were at least thirty leagues distant from it; the sky it is true, was extremely clear.

The commander resolved to send a boat to St. Croix, one of the principal towns in the island, to fetch fruits, and some filtering stones, which are made in that town; they are only a kind of mortar, made of the volcanic stone of the country. In consequence, during the whole night we made short tacks; the next morning we coasted the island, at the distance of two musket shot, and passed under the guns of a little fort, called *Fort Français*. One of our companions leaped for joy, at the sight of this little fort, which was raised in haste by a few Frenchmen, when the English, under Admiral Nelson, attempted to take possession of the Colony. It was there, said he, that a numerous fleet, commanded by one of the bravest Admirals of the

English navy, failed before a handful of French, who covered themselves with glory and saved Teneriffe; the Admiral was obliged to take flight, after having lost an arm in the contest, which was long and obstinate.

Having doubled a point which extends into the sea, we entered the bay, at the bottom of which is the town of St. Croix. The appearance of Teneriffe is majestic: the whole island is composed of mountains, which are extremely high, and crowned with rocks terrifying from their size, which on the north side, seem to rise perpendicularly above the surface of the ocean, and to threaten every moment to crush by their fall, the vessels which pass near their base. Above them all rises the Pico, the summit of which is lost in the clouds. We did not perceive that the Pic was constantly covered with snow as som voyagers affirm, nor that it vomits forth lava of melted metal; for when we observed it, its summit seemed intirely destitute of snow and of volcanic eruptions. At the foot of the mountain, and up to a certain elevation excavations filled with sulphur are observed; and in its neighbourhood several of the sepulchral caverns of the Guanches, the ancient inhabitants of the island.

Towards noon the *Echo* corvette, which had parted company, rejoined us, and passed under the stern of the frigate: she was ordered to imitate our manœuvres, which she instantly did; she did not send any boat on shore. Thus united, we lay to together in the bay of St. Croix. About four o'clock in the afternoon, the boat having returned on board we directed our course for Senegal. They had bought in the town some earthen jars of a large size, precious wines, oranges, lemons, banian figs, and vegetables of all kinds.

Several unfortunate Frenchmen were on the island who had been long prisoners of war; they lived upon what the Spaniards chose to give them. They had been restored to liberty on the conclusion of peace, and waited only for a favorable opportunity to return to France. Their entreaties to the officer who commanded the boat were useless; he had the cruelty to refuse to restore them to their country and their families. In this boat there was another officer M. Laperère, who strongly insisted on bringing away these unfortunate persons; his entreaties could not move him who commanded the boat.

The depravity of morals at St. Croix is extreme; so much so that when the women heard that some Frenchmen were arrived in the town, they placed themselves at their doors, and when they passed, urged them to enter. All this is usually done in the presence of the husbands, who have no right to oppose it, because the Holy Inquisition will have it so, and because the monks who are very numerous in the island take care that this custom is observed. They possess the art of blinding the husbands, by means of the *prestiges* of religion, which they abuse in the highest degree; they cure them of their jealousy, to which they are much inclined, by assuring them that their passion, which they call ridiculous, or conjugal mania, is nothing but the persecution of Satan which torments them, and from which they alone are able to deliver them, by inspiring their dear consorts with some religious sentiments. These abuses are almost inevitable in a burning climate, where the passion of love is often stronger than reason, and sometimes breaks through the barriers which religion attempts to oppose to it: this depravity of morals must therefore be attributed to inflamed passions, and not to abuses facilitated by a religion so sublime as ours.

The Island of Teneriffe is not equal to that of Madeira: one cannot even compare their agricultural productions, on account of the great difference of their soils: but in a commercial view, Teneriffe has the advantage of Madeira. Its geographical position in the middle of the Canaries, enables it to carry on an extensive trade, while Madeira is confined to the sale aud exchange of its wines for articles of European manufacture.

The soil of Teneriffe is much drier; a great part of it is too volcanic to be used for agriculture: every part of it however, which is capable of producing anything is very well cultivated, which should seem to prove, that the Spaniards of this country are naturally much less indolent than they have been represented.

When we were in the open sea we had favorable winds from the N. N. E.

In the night of the 29th of June the frigate caught fire between decks, by the negligence of the master baker; but being discovered in time, the fire was extinguished. In the following night the same accident was repeated; but this time it was necessary, in order to stop the progress of the fire, to pull down the oven which was rebuilt the next day.

On the 1st of July we descried Cape Bayados, situated in latitude 26° 12′ 30″, and in longitude 16° 47′. We then saw the skirts of the immense desert of Zaara, and we thought we perceived the mouth of the river St. John, which is very little known. We passed the tropic at ten o'clock in the morning; the usual ceremony was there performed with a certain pomp; the jokes of the sailors amused us for some moments; we were far from thinking of the cruel event which was soon to deprive of their lives a third of the persons who were on board the frigate. This custom of tropical baptism is strange enough; the chief object of it, is, to procure the sailors some money.

From St. Croix, we had constantly steered to the S.S.W. During the ceremony at the tropic we doubled Cape Barbas, situated in lat. 22_0 6′, and long. 19^0 8′: two officers suddenly had the course changed, without informing the captain; this led to a pretty warm dispute, which however had no serious consequences. These two officers affirmed that we were running upon a group of rocks, and that we were already very near to the breakers. We had sailed the whole morning in the Gulph of St. Cyprian, the bottom of which is strewed with rocks, so that at low water, brigantines cannot frequent these seas, as we were told at Senegal by M. Valentin, senior, who is perfectly acquainted with this whole coast, and could not conceive how the frigate could have passed amidst all these reefs without striking. The shore was within half a cannon shot, and we clearly saw enormous rocks over which the sea broke violently.* If it had fallen calm, there is no doubt but the strong currents which set, in-shore, would have infallibly carried us into danger.

In the evening we thought we descried Cape Blanco, and according to the instructions given by the Navy Office, we steered W.S.W. During a part of the night the *Echo*, with which we had constantly kept company since we left Madeira, burnt several charges of powder and hung a lanthorn at the mizen-mast; her signals were not answered in the same manner; only a lanthorn was hung for a few moments to the fore-mast; it went out soon after, and was not replaced by another light. M. Savigny was on deck

---

* This route was not recommended by the instructions, but there was on board an old sea officer, who announced himself as a pilot in these seas; his advice was unfortunately attended to.

where he remained a part of the night: he had full opportunity to perceive the negligence of the officer of the watch, who did not even deign to answer the signals made by the *Echo*. Why, in the neighbourhood of so formidable a danger, not compare the points of the two ships, as is usual when vessels sail in company? The captain of the frigate was not even informed of the signals of the corvette. At eleven o'clock, she bore off the larboard bow; and soon after he perceived that the direction of her course made a pretty large angle with ours, and that it tended to cross us passing a-head; he soon perceived her on the starboard: it is affirmed that her journal states that she sailed the whole night W.S.W. ours does the same. We must necessarily have hauled to the larboard, or she to the starboard, since at day-break the corvette was no longer in sight.

At sea a vessel may easily be perceived at the distance of six leagues. From midnight till six in the morning, she must have gained above six leagues of us, which is not to be imagined, for she sailed much slower than we and stopped every two hours to take soundings. To explain this separation we must necessarily admit either that the frigate steered more south, or the corvette more west, if the two vessels had run on the same tack it would be impossible to explain it.

Every two hours the frigate brought-to, to sound; every half hour the lead was cast without lowering the sails; we were always upon shallows, and stood out to sea, to find a greater quantity of water: at length about six o'clock in the morning we had above a hundred fathoms; we then stood-to the S. S. E.; this course made almost a right angle with that which we had followed in the night: it bore directly in-shore, the approach to which, in this place, is rendered terrible by a very long reef, called Arguin, which according to instructions we had on board extends above thirty leagues in breadth.*

---

* A description of the reef of Arguin may be found in the *Little Sea Torch*.

According to the instructions given by the Minister of the Marine, this danger is avoided by running only twenty-two leagues in the open sea; it is true they recommend not to approach the shore but with the greatest precaution, and with the sounding line in the hand : the other ships of the expedition which sailed according to those instructions all arrived at St. Louis without any accident, which is a certain proof of their exactness.* Besides it is said, that one must make W. S. W., when one has discerned Cape Blanco; and it is probable we had not got sight of it in the evening, as was supposed. We therefore had an uncertain point of departure; hence the error which was so fatal to us.

According to my Comrade Correard, we cannot pass over in silence, a scene which took place in the morning.

---

* Besides the instructions given by the Minister, for sailing, after having made Cape Blanco, there was a letter sent some days before our departure from the road of the Isle of Aix, recommending the commander of the expedition not to depend upon the Charts, upon which the reef is very erroneously placed.

The Captain was deceived in the most singular manner; about five or six o'clock he was called up; some persons who were on deck persuaded him that a great cloud which was in the direction of Cape Blanco and in truth very near it, was that Cape itself. My companion in misfortune, who sees clearly, and who knows how to distinguish between a rock and a cloud, because he has seen enough of them in the Alps, where he was born, told those gentlemen that it was only a cape of vapour; he was answered that the instructions which the minister had given to the captain prescribed to him to make this cape; but that we had passed it above ten leagues; that at this moment the question was, to make the captain believe that the instructions of the minister had been punctually followed, and that they desired to persuade him, which was not difficult, that this cloud was the Cape. Many have deposed, as we have been told, that Cape Blanco, had been seen in the evening of the 1st of July: we venture to affirm that that rock was not seen at all.

After this pretended reconnoissance of the 2d July, if we were persuaded that we had seen that Cape, we should have steered west, to double the bank of Arguin; the danger once passed, the course should have been again directed to the south which is the route to Senegal; but he who for some days past had guided the course of the ship, thought proper to persuade the captain, to take immediately the southerly course, and to steer for Portendic. We are ignorant of the reasons which induced the commander of the frigate to give his confidence to a man who did not belong to the staff. He was an ex-officer of the marine, who had just left an English prison, where he had been for ten years; he certainly had not acquired there knowledge superior to that of the officers on board, whom this mark of deference could not but offend. M. de Chaumareys, while we were doubling Cape Barbas, presided at the farce performed in passing the Tropic, while he who had gained his confidence, was walking up and down the deck of the frigate, coolly observing the numerous dangers, spread along the coast. Several persons remonstrated against this management of the vessel, particularly Mr. Picard the greffier of Senegal, who had struck upon the bank of Arguin eight years before; this enlightened man declared at that time that we were running into danger.

As soon as the sun's altitude was observed to ascertain our position, we saw, on the quarter deck, Mr. Maudet, ensign of the watch, working the day's work, (making out the reckoning) upon a chicken coop; this officer who knows all the duties of his profession, affirmed that we were on the edge of the reef; he communicated this to the person who for some days past had given his counsel to the commander respecting the course to be steered; he received for answer; never mind, we are in eighty fathoms*

---

* Mr. Lapérère, the officer on the watch before Mr. Maudet, found by his reckoning, that we were very near the reef; he was not listened to, though he did his utmost, at least to ascertain our situation by sounding. We have mentioned the names of Messrs. Lapérere and Maudet, because if they had been attended to, the Medusa would be still in existence.

If our course during the night had partly averted all our dangers, that which was taken in the morning led us into them again. Mr. Maudet, convinced that we were upon the reef, took upon him, to have soundings taken; the colour of the water was intirely changed, which was observed even by those who were the least used to recognise the depth of the sea, by the appearance of the water; we even thought that we saw sand roll amid the little waves that rose; numerous sea weeds were seen by the ship's side, and a great many fish were caught. All these facts proved indubitably that we were on shallow water: in fact the lead announced only eighteen fathoms; the officer of the watch immediately informed the captain, who gave orders to come a little more to the wind; we were going before the wind the studding sails on the larboard; these sails were immediately lowered; the lead was again cast, and showed six fathoms; the captain gave orders to haul the wind as close as possible, but unhappily it was too late.

The frigate luffing, almost immediately gave a heel; it proceeded a moment longer; gave a second and then a third; it stopped at a place where the sounding line showed only a depth of five metres sixty centimetres, and it was the time of high water.

Unhappily we were in the season of the high tides, which was the most unfavorable time for us because they were going to decline, and we ran a ground just when the water was at the highest; for the rest, the tides do not much differ in these seas; at the time of full moon they do not rise more than fifty centimetres more than usual; in the spring tides the water does not rise above one hundred and twenty centimetres on the reef. We have already said that when we grounded, the sounding line marked only five metres, and sixty centimetres; and at low water it marked, four metres sixty centimetres, the frigate therefore saved by a metre: however, as soon as we had stranded, the boats which went out to sound, met with places deeper than that, where we struck, and many others not so deep; which made us suppose that the reef is very uneven and covered with little elevations. All the different manœuvres which had been performed since the moment when we found ourselves in eighteen fathoms, to that in which we struck, succeeded each other with extraordinary rapidity: not above ten minutes passed. Several persons have assured us that, if the ship had come entirely to the wind, when we were in eighteen fathoms, the frigate might perhaps have got clean, for she did not run wholly aground till she got to the west part of the reef, and upon its edge.

We stranded on the 2d of July, at a quarter after three p. m. in 19° 36′ north latitude, and 19° 45′ west longitude. This event spread the most profound consternation; if in the midst of this disorder, there were any men who remained collected enough to make observations, they must have been struck with the extraordinary changes impressed on every countenance; some persons were not to be recognised.

D

Here you might see features become shrunk and hideous; there a countenance which had assumed a yellow and even a greenish hue, some men seemed thunderstruck and chained down to their places, without strength to move. When they had recovered from the stupefaction, with which they were at first seized, numbers gave themselves up to excess of despair; while others uttered imprecations upon those whose ignorance had been so fatal to us. An officer going upon deck, immediately after the accident, spoke with energy to him, who, as we have already said, had directed for some days the course of the ship, and said to him, "*See, Sir, to what your obstinacy has brought us; I had warned you of it.*" Two women alone seemed insensible to this disaster; they were the wife and daughter of the governor. What a shocking contrast! men who for twenty or twenty-five years, had been exposed to a thousand dangers, were profoundly affected, while Madame and Mademoiselle Chemals, appeared insensible, and as if unconcerned in these events.

As soon as the frigate stranded, the sails were hastily lowered, the top gallant masts got down, the top masts lowered, and every thing necessary arranged to get her off the reef. After numerous efforts, night being come, they were suspended to give some repose to the crew, who had displayed extreme activity. The next day, the third, the top masts were got down, the yards lowered, and they heaved at the capstern upon an anchor which had been fixed the evening before, at a cable's length a-stern of the frigate. This operation was fruitless; for the anchor, which was too weak, could not make sufficient resistance and gave way: a bower anchor was then used, which, after infinite pains, was carried out to a considerable distance, to a place where there was only a depth of five metres sixty centimetres; in order to carry it so far, it was fixed behind a boat, under which was placed a number of empty barrels fastened together, because the boat was not able to carry so considerable a weight.* The sea ran very high, and the current was extremely strong.

This boat, when it reached the spot where it was to cast the anchor, could not place it in the proper position to make the flukes fix in the sand, for one of the extremities already touched the bottom, while the other was still out of the water: being thus ill fixed, it could not answer the purpose intended; when they began to heave upon it, it made very little resistance, and would have been dragged on board again if they had continued to work at the capstern.† In the course of the day, we staved several water butts which were in the hold, and pumped immediately, the top masts, except the small one which could not be got down, were thrown into the sea; the yards, the boom, and all the pieces of wood which afterwards composed

---

* This was not the long boat of the frigate; it was a boat in no very good condition, which was to be left at Senegal, for the service of the port.

† The bottom was besides soft; being sand mixed with grey mud, and shells.

the raft, were also put over board : the two lower yards were retained in their place, to serve as shores to the frigate, and to support it, in case it threatened to upset.

If the loss of the vessel was certain, it was proper to secure the escape of the crew : a council was called, at which the governor of Senegal gave the plan of a raft, capable, it was said, of carrying two hundred men, with provisions.* It was necessary to have recourse to an expedient of this nature, because our six boats were judged to be incapable of taking on board four hundred men, which was our number. The provisions were to be deposited on the raft, and at the hours of meals, the crews of the boats would have come to receive their rations : we were to reach all together the sandy coast of the desert, and there furnished with arms and ammunition, which were to be taken in by the boats before we left the frigate, we were to form a caravan, and proceed to

* This plan was shewn to several persons; we ourselves saw it in the hands of the governor, who sketched it, leaning on the geat capstern.

the Island of St. Louis. The events which happened in the sequel, proved that this plan was perfectly well laid, and that it might have been crowned with success: unhappily these decisions were traced upon a loose sand, which was dispersed by the breath of egotism.

In the evening another anchor was cast, at a pretty considerable distance from the frigate: just before high water, we began to work at the capstern, but in vain. The work was put off till the next morning's tide; during all this time, the operations were performed with the greatest difficulty; the sea was hollow, the winds strong, the boats which had to go to a distance either to sound or fix anchors, could not attain their object, without the greatest efforts; rapid currents, added to the difficulties. If the weather had not been so extremely unfavorable to us, perhaps the frigate might have been got afloat the next day, for it had been resolved to carry out very long warps, but the violence of the wind, and the sea, baffled these arrangements which nothing but a calm could favor. The weather was bad during the whole night; about four or five o'clock, at the morning tide, all our efforts to raise her were still fruitless; we began to despair of even being able to save her from this danger; the boats were repaired, and the construction of the raft diligently prosecuted: during the day of the 4. several barrels of flour were thrown into the sea, some water casks staved; some barrels of powder, intended as articles to trade with Segenal, were also got overboard.

In the evening, a few minutes before high water, the labours at the capstern recommenced; this time the anchors did not deceive our expectations; for, after a few moments labour, the frigate moved on the larboard; this motion was effected by means of an anchor fixed on the north west; the stream cable which was bent to its ring, came by the head of the ship and tended to make it swing; while another much stronger one, the cable of which passed through one of the stern ports, tended to prevent it from running a-head, by supporting its quarters the motions of which were commanded by means of this force. This first success gave us great hopes; we worked with ardor.

After some further efforts, the *Medusa* began to swing sensibly; we redoubled our efforts, she swung intirely and then had her head turned to the open sea. She was almost afloat, only her stern touched a little; the work could not be continued, because the anchor was too near, and it would have been hove up. If a warp had been carried out in the open sea, by continuing to haul upon it, the frigate would have been got wholly afloat that evening. All the things which had been thrown overboard had lightened her by twenty or thirty centimetres at the most, her draught of water might certainly have been lessened still more; but it was not done because the Governor of Senegal objected to throwing the barrels of flour into the sea, alledging that the greatest scarcity prevailed in the European factories. These considerations, however, should not have caused it to be overlooked that we had on board fourteen twenty-four pounders, and that it would have been easy to throw them overboard, and send them even to a considerable distance from the frigate, by means of the yard tackle; besides, the flour barrels might have been carefully fastened together, and when we were once out of danger, it would have been easy for us to remove them. This plan might have been executed without any fear of doing much damage to the flour, which when it is plunged in the water forms round the inside of the barrel a pretty thick crust, in consequence of the moisture, so that the interior is preserved from injury: this method was indeed attempted, but it was given up, because the means employed were insufficient. More care should have been used, and all the difficulties would have been conquered; only half measures were adopted, and in all the manœuvres great want of decision prevailed.

If the frigate had been lightened as

soon as we struck, perhaps she might have been saved.* The weather, however, as we have already said, was almost always unfavourable, and often hindered the operations.

Some persons expected to see the frigate got afloat the next day, and their joy shewed that they were fully persuaded of it: there were indeed some probabilities, but they were very slight; for the vessel had been merely got out of its bed. We had hardly succeeded in changing its place to a distance of about two hundred metres, when the sea began to ebb: the frigate rested on the sand, which obliged us to suspend for ever our last operations. If it had been possible to hold her this night to two or three cables more in the open sea, still lightening her, perhaps, we repeat it, she might have been placed out of danger.

---

* Two officers displayed the greatest activity, they would have thrown into the sea every thing that could be got overboard. They were permitted to proceed for a moment; and the next moment contrary orders were given.

At night the sky became cloudy, the winds came from the sea, and blew violently. The sea ran high, and the frigate began to heel with more and more violence, every moment we expected to see her bulge; consternation again spread, and we soon felt the cruel certainty that she was irrecoverably lost. She bulged in the middle of the night, the keel broke in two, the helm was unship'd, and held to the stern only by the chains, which caused it to do dreadful damage; it produced the effect of a strong horizontal ram, which violently impelled by the waves, continually struck the poop of the ship; the whole back part of the captain's cabin was beat in, the water entered in an alarming manner. About eleven o'clock there was a kind of mutiny, which was afterwards checked by the presence of the governor and the officers; it was excited by some soldiers, who persuaded their comrades that it was intended to abandon them on board the frigate, while the crew escaped in the boats; these alarms were excited by the imprudence of a young man; some soldiers had already taken their arms, and had ranged themselves on the deck, all the avenues to which they occupied.

The raft, impelled by the strength of the current and of the sea, broke the cable which fastened it to the frigate and began to drive; those who beheld this accident announced it by their cries, and a boat was immediately sent after it, which brought it back. This was a distressing night for us all; agitated by the idea that our frigate was totally lost, and alarmed by the violent shocks which it received from the waves, we were unable to take a moment's repose.

At day-break, on the 5th, there were two metres seventy centimetres water in the hold, and the pumps could no longer work with effect: it was decided we ought to quit the vessel as soon as possible. The frigate, it was said, threatened to upset; a childish fear, doubtless; but, what particularly made it absolutely necessary to abandon her, was, that the water had already penetrated between decks. A quantity of biscuit was hastily taken from the store-room; wine and fresh water were also got out; these provisions were intended to be placed in the boats and on the raft. To preserve the biscuit from the salt water it was put into strong iron hooped barrels, which were perfectly fit for the purpose. We are ignorant why these provisions, so carefully prepared were not embarked either on the raft or in the boats; the precipitation with which we embarked was the cause of this negligence, so that some boats did not save above twenty-four pounds of biscuit, a small cask of water and very little wine: the rest was abandoned on the deck of the frigate or thrown into the sea during the tumult of the evacuation. The raft alone had a pretty large quantity of wine, but not a single barrel of biscuit, and if any was put upon it, it was thrown off by the soldiers when they placed themselves upon it. To avoid confusion, there was made, the day before, a list of the persons who were to embark, assigning to every one the post he was to occupy;

but no attention was paid to this wise arrangement; every one took the means which he thought the most favorable to reach the shore; those who executed the orders which they had received to place themselves on the raft, had certainly reason to repent it. Mr. Savigny was unfortunately of this number; he might have stopped on board a boat, but an invincible attachment to his duty made him forget the danger of the part which was allotted him.

At length, the moment when we were to abandon the frigate arrived. First, the soldiers were embarked, who were almost all placed upon the raft: they wanted to take their muskets and some cartridges: this was formally opposed.* They left them on the deck, and preserved only their sabres: some few, however, saved their carbines, and, almost all the officers, their fowling pieces and pistols. In all, we were about one hundred and forty-seven or one hundred and fifty; such is pretty nearly the account of the persons

---
* Why was it opposed?

who embarked on this fatal machine, one hundred and twenty soldiers, including the officers of the army, twenty-nine men, sailors and passengers, and one woman. The barge, commanded by a lieutenant, on board of which were the governor and his family, took in thirty-five persons in all: this large fourteen-oared vessel, could certainly have carried a larger number: besides the people, there were three trunks; another fourteen-oared boat took in forty-two persons; the captain's barge took twenty-eight; the long boat, though in a very bad condition, destitute of oars, took in, however, eighty-eight; an eight-oared boat which was to be left at Senegal, for the service of the port, took twenty-five sailors; the smallest of the boats had fifteen persons on board; among whom were the interesting family of Mr. Picard, of whom we have spoken above: it was composed of three young ladies, his wife, and four young children. All these numbers added together, form a total of three hundred and ninety-seven persons;* there were on board the frigate, near four hundred sailors and soldiers: thus it appears that several poor wretches were abandoned; when the Medusa was again found, fifty-two days after, it was ascertained that the number of those, who had been abandoned, was seventeen; which proves to us, that there were more than one hundred and forty seven of us on the raft, and that it is more correct to fix the number of the men at a hundred and fifty. It is said, that when the last boat, which was the long boat, left the frigate, several men refused to embark in her; the others were too mnch intoxicated to think of their safety. A man of the name of Dalès, one of the seventeen who remained on board the frigate, deposed in the council, that fourteen men had left the long boat, because they did not think it capable of carrying so many, and that he, with two

---

* The numbers above mentioned make only three hundred and eighty-three, so that there is an error somewhere.   T.

others hid themselves, that they might not be compelled to go on board. We are ignorant of the depositions of his two companions.

What a sight was it to behold a multitude of wretches, who all wanted to escape death, and all sought to save themselves, either in the boats or upon the rafts! The frigate's ladder was insufficient for so many: some threw themselves from the vessels, trusting to the end of a rope, which was scarcely able to bear a man's weight; some fell into the sea, and were recovered; what is surprising is, that amidst all this confusion, there was not a single serious accident.

Though in so terrible a situation, on our fatal raft, we cast our eyes upon the frigate, and deeply regretted this fine vessel, which, a few days before, seemed to command the waves, which it cut through with astonishing rapidity. The masts, which had supported immense sails, no longer existed, the barricade was entirely destroyed: the vessel itself was cast on the larboard quarter.

E

All the boats, after they had sheered off, proceeded in different manners, as we shall afterwards relate; but the men on board, when they reached the shore, had to contend with a thousand causes of destruction. We will first exactly relate all the operations that were executed till the moment when the raft was abandoned.

About seven o'clock, the signal for departure was given; four of the boats stood out to sea, the raft was still along side of the frigate, where it was moored: the captain's barge was under the bowsprit, and the barge near our machine, on which it had just embarked some men. At length we were ordered to depart; but whether from a presentiment of what was to happen to us, or whether Mr. Correard entertained just fears, which the event proved to be but too well founded, he would not depart, till he had convinced himself that our raft was provided with all the necessary instruments and charts, to navigate with some degree of safety, in case bad weather should oblige the boats to separate from us. As it was impossible to move upon the raft, because we were so crowded together, he thought it the easiest to call to Mr. . . . . who immediately answered to his call. Coming to the larboard, he asked what we wanted? The following questions were then put to him: " Are we in a condition to depart? Have we instruments and charts?" Yes, yes, replied he, " I have provided you with every thing that can be necessary for you." He was then asked, what naval officer was to come and command us? he answered: " It is I; in a moment I shall be with you." After saying this he disappeared, and went on board one of the boats.

How is it possible that a French sea officer should be guilty of such bad faith to his unhappy countrymen, who placed all their confidence in him?

At last, the barge came to the head of the frigate, and the governor caused himself to be let down in an arm chair; it then threw a tow rope to our raft, and we stood off with this one boat; the second boat then gave a tow line to the first; the

Senegal boat came afterwards, and did the same; there remained three boats, the captain's, which was still at the head of the frigate, on board of which last there were above eighty men, who uttered cries of despair, when they saw the boats and the raft stand off. The three boats which towed us, soon brought us to a distance from the vessel; they had a good wind, and the sailors rowed like men who were resolved to save themselves from the imminent danger which threatened us. The long-boat, and the pinnace were at some distance, and attempted to return on board; lastly, M. De Chaumareys embarked in his barge, by one of the ropes a-head: some sailors threw themselves into it, and loosened the ropes, by which it was lashed to the frigate. Immediately the cries of the people who remained on board redoubled, and an officer of the troops even took up a carbine to fire at the captain : but was prevented. We soon saw that this man was not equal to his duty ; from the manner in which he abandoned his people. We regretted that the arm of the officer had been withheld when he wished to prevent the captain's design; but, our regret was unavailing; the mischief was done; it was irreparable; he had no idea of repairing it, and he could not return on board, for he was sure to meet there with that death, which he sought to avoid, at the expence of honor.

M. de Chaumareys, however, went on board the long-boat, and gave order that it should take in the men who remained on board the frigate. Some persons belonging to this boat have informed us, that they were told there were, at the most, about twenty who could not embark; but, the long-boat, destitute of oars, attempted, to no purpose, to get back to the frigate; a boat tried, without success, to tow it; it could not attain the object, till it sent the pinnace to fetch some long ropes, one end of which was lashed to the frigate, and the other brought on board the long-boat, which was thus towed to the larboard side of the ship. Lieutenant Espiau, who commanded this large boat, was surprised at finding above sixty soldiers and sailors, instead of twenty. This officer went on board with Mr. Bredif, engineer of mines, who tried to recall to their reason, those whose intellectual faculties had been impaired by the presence of danger. Mr. Espiau, embarked with proper order, the men who were on the deck; seventeen only as we have said, refused; some fearing that the boat would founder before she could reach the raft, and the other boats, which left it more and more behind; some others, because they were too much intoxicated as we have stated, to think of their safety. The fears of the former, (and they are probably those who, according to the deposition of Dalès, returned on board the frigate) were founded on the bad condition of the long-boat, which let in the water on every side. After promising the men who persisted in remaining, that assistance should be sent them, as soon as the others arrived at Senegal, the long-boat stood off to join the little division. Before he left the frigate, Mr. Espiau had the grand national flag hoisted.

When this boat left the frigate to join us, we were, at least, a league and a half distant; the captain's barge had come some time before to take the towrope, and was at the head of the line; the smallest of the boats (the pinnace) did not take the towline; it preceded the little division, probably to take soundings.

As soon as all the boats had taken their post, cries of "*Vive le Roi!*" were a thousand times repeated by the men upon the raft, and a little white flag was hoisted at the top of a musket. Such was the order of the boats and the raft. The chiefs of the little division which was to conduct us to the land, had sworn not to abandon us: we are far from accusing all those gentlemen of having violated the laws of honor; but a series of circumstances obliged them to renounce the generous plan which they had formed to save us, or to perish with us. These circumstances deserve to be scrupulously examined; but our pen, guided by truth, must not fear to record facts which truth itself dictates. It is true they are of so strange a nature, that it is unpleasant to make them known. It is painful to us, to have to recount such events: we have to shew to what a degree the imagination of man is susceptible of being struck by the presence of danger, so as to make him even forget the duties which honour imposes on him. We, doubtless, admit that in forsaking the raft, the minds of those who did so, were greatly agitated, and that the desire of withdrawing themselves from danger, made them forget that a hundred and fifty unfortunate men were going to be abandoned to the most cruel sufferings. We shall relate the facts as we observed them, and as they have been communicated to us, by some of our companions in misfortune.

Before we proceed, we will describe the construction of this raft, to which a hundred and fifty persons were entrusted.

It was composed of the top-masts of the frigate, yards, fishes, boom, &c. These different pieces joined together by very strong ropes, were perfectly solid; the two principal pieces were two top-masts, which were placed at the extremity of the two sides; four other masts, two of which were of the same length and strength as the first, joined two by two, at the center of the machine, added to its solidity. The other pieces were placed within these four first but were not equal to them in length. Boards were nailed on this first foundation, and formed a kind of parapet, which would have been of great service to us if it had been higher. To render our raft still more solid, long pieces of wood had been placed across, which projected at least three metres: on the sides, there was a kind of railing, but it was not above forty centimetres in height: it would have been easy to add some crotches to it, which would have formed a breast-work of sufficient height; but it was not done, probably because those who had the machine built, were not to be exposed upon it. To the ends of the top-masts, two top-gallant yards were lashed, the farther ends of which were bound by a very strong cord, and thus formed the front part of the raft. The angular space, formed by the two yards, was filled with pieces of wood laid across, and planks ill adjusted. This fore part, which was at least two metres in length, had very little solidity, and was continually submerged. The hinder part did not terminate in a point like the fore part, but a considerable length of this part was not more solid, so that in fact, there was only the center which was really to be depended upon: an example will enable the reader to judge of its dimensions. When we were no more than fifteen in it, we had not space enough to lie down, and yet we were extremely close together. The raft, from one extremity, to the other was at least twenty metres in length, and about seven in breadth; this length might induce one to think, at the first sight, that it was able to carry two hundred men, but we soon had cruel proofs of its weakness. It was without sails or mast. As we left the frigate they threw us the fore-top-gallant and the main-top-gallant sails; but they did it with such precipitation, that, some persons who were at their post, were in danger of being wounded by the fall of these sails, which were bent to the yards. They did not give us any ropes to set up our mast.

There was on board the raft a great quantity of barrels of flour, which had been deposited there the preceding day, not to serve for provisions during the passage, from the frigate to the coast, but because the raft, formed of the barrels, not having succeeded, they were deposited on the machine, that they might not be carried away by the sea, there were also six barrels of wine and two small casks of water, which had been put there for the use of the people.

Scarcely fifty men had got upon the raft, when it sunk at least seventy centimetres under water; so that to facilitate the embarkation of the other soldiers it was necessary to throw into the sea all the flour barrels, which lifted by the waves, began to float and were violently driven against the men who were at their post; if they had been fixed, perhaps some of them might have been saved: as it was, we saved only the wine and the water, because several persons united to preserve them, and had much difficulty to hinder them from being thrown into the sea like the flour barrels. The raft, lightened by throwing away these barrels, was able to receive more men; we were at length a hundred and fifty. The machine was submerged at least a metre: we were so crowded together that it was impossible to take a single step; at the back and the front, we were in water up to the middle. At the moment that we were putting off from the frigate, a bag with twenty-five pounds of biscuit was thrown us, which fell into the sea; we got it up with difficulty; it was converted into a paste, but we preserved it in that condition. Several considerate persons fastened the casks of wine and water to the cross pieces of the raft, and we kept a strict watch over them. Thus we have faithfully described the nature of our situation when we put off from the vessel.

The Commander of the raft was named Coudin who was, what is called in the French marine an *Aspirant* of the first class. Some days before our departure from the roads of the Isle of Aix, he had received a severe contusion on the fore part of the right leg, which was not approaching to its cure, when we stranded and wholly incapacitated him from moving. One of his comrades, moved by his situation, offered to take his place, but Mr. Coudin, though wounded, preferred repairing to the dangerous post which was assigned him, because he was the oldest officer of his class on board. He was hardly on board the raft, when the sea water so increased the pain in his leg, that he nearly fainted; we gave notice of his situation to the nearest boat, we were answered that a boat would come and fetch this officer. I do not know whether the order was given, but it is certain that Mr. Coudin was obliged to remain on the fatal raft.

The long-boat, which we have been forced to lose sight of for a moment, in order to give these necessary details, at length rallied; it was, as we have stated, the last that left the frigate. The lieutenant who commanded her, justly fearing that he should not be able to keep the sea, in a crazy boat destitute of oars, badly rigged, and making much water, ran along-side of the first boat, begging it to take in some men; they refused. This long boat was to leave us some ropes to fix our mast; which an instant before had been hauled to us, by the first boat, which we had before us: we do not know what reason hindered it from leaving us these ropes, but it passed on, and ran along-side the second boat, which equally refused to take any body on board. The officer, who commanded the long-boat, seeing that they refused to take any of his men, and falling more and more under the wind, because his sails were badly trimmed, and the currents drove him, made up to the third boat, commanded by a sub-lieutenant named Maudet; this officer, commanding a slight boat which the day before had a plank beat in, by one of the cross pieces of the raft, (an accident which had been remedied by covering the hole with a large piece of lead,) and being besides heavily laden, in order to avoid the shock of the long-boat, which might have been fatal to him, was forced to let loose the towrope, which held him to the barge, and thus broke in two the line formed by the boats before the raft, by separating himself from it with the captains boat which was at the head: when the captain and Mr. Maudet had disengaged themselves they hauled the wind, and then put about to come and take their post; Mr. Maudet, even hailed M. de Chaumareys, *" Captain take your towrope again,"* he received for answer, *yes my friend*. Two boats were still at their post, but before the other two were able to rejoin them, the barge separated itself; the officer who commanded it, expressed himself as follows respecting his thus abandoning us. " The towrope was not let go from " my boat, but from that behind me." This second desertion was the forerunner of another still more cruel; for the officer who commanded the last boat in which was the governor, after having towed us alone, for a moment, caused the rope to be loosened which held it to the raft. When the towropes were let go, we were two leagues from the frigate; the breeze came from the sea, which was as favorable as could be desired. This last towrope did not break, as the governor has tried to persuade the minister of the marine, and several persons who escaped from the raft. Walking on the terrace of a French merchant at Senegal, in the presence of Messrs. Savigny and Coudin, the governor explained the affair as follows: " Some men were on the front of the raft, " at the place where the tow-rope was " fixed, which they pulled so as to draw " the boat nearer to them; they had al- " ready pulled several fathoms of it to " them, but a wave coming, gave a vio- " lent shock; these men were obliged to " let go: the boats then proceeded more " rapidly, till the rope was stretched; at " the moment when the boats effected " this tension the effort was such, that " the rope broke." This manner of explaining this last desertion is very adroit, and might easily deceive those who were not on the spot, but it is not possible for us to accede to it, since we could even name the person who loosened it.

Some persons belonging to the other boats have assured us, that all the boats were coming to resume their post, when a cry of "*we forsake them,*" was heard: we have this fact from many of our companions in misfortune. The whole line was thrown into disorder, and no measures were taken to remedy it: it is probable, that if one of the first officers had set the example, order would have been restored; but every one was left to himself; hence there was no concert in the little division; every one thought of escaping from personal danger.

Let us here do justice to the courage of Mr. Clanet, pay-master of the frigate, who was on board the governor's boat; if he had been listened to, this tow-rope would not have been let go; every moment an officer who was in the governor's boat cried out aloud, "*shall I let go?*" Mr. Clanet opposed it, answering with firmness, "*No no!*" Some persons joined him, but could obtain nothing, the tow-rope was let go: we considered it as certain, that the commander of the other boats, on seeing the chief of the expedition courageously devote himself, would have come and resumed their posts : but it may be said that each individual boat was abandoned by all the others: there was wanting, on this occasion, a man of great coolness: and ought not this man to have been found among the chief officers ? How shall their conduct be justified? There are, certainly, some reasons to be alledged. Impartial judges of events, we will describe them, not as unhappy victims of the consequences of this desertion, but as men free from all personal resentment, and who listen only to the voice of truth.

The raft, drawn by all the boats united, dragged them a little back; it is true that we just had the ebb, and the currents set from shore. To be in the open sea with undecked vessels, might well inspire some apprehensions: but, in a few hours, the currents would change and favor us; we ought to have waited for this moment, which would have infallibly demonstrated the possibility of drawing us to the coast, which was not above twelve or fifteen leagues distant: this is so true that the boats discovered the coast, the same evening, before sunset. Perhaps they would have been forced to forsake us the second night after our departure, if indeed more than thirty-six hours had been required to tow us to land; for the weather was very bad; but we should then have been very near to the coast, and it would have been very easy to save us: at least we should have had only the elements to accuse!—We are persuaded that a short time would have sufficed to tow us within sight of land, for, the evening of our being deserted, the raft was precisely in the direction which the boats had followed between the frigates and the coast, and, at least, five leagues from the former. The next morning, at daybreak, we could no longer see the Medusa.(14)

At the first moment we did not really believe that we had been so cruelly abandoned. We imagined that the boats had let loose, because they had perceived a vessel, and hastened towards it to ask assistance. The long-boat was pretty near us to leeward on the starboard. She lowered her foresail half way down: her manœuvre made us think that she was going to take the first tow-rope: she remained so a moment, lowered her foresail entirely, set up her main-mast, hoisted her sails, and followed the rest of the division. Some men in this boat, seeing that the others deserted us, threatened to fire upon them, but were stopped by Lieutenant Espiau. Many persons have assured us that it was the intention of this officer to come and take the tow-rope; but his crew opposed it; had he done so, he would certainly have acted with great imprudence. His efforts would have been of little use to us, and his devotedness would but have increased the number of victims.(15) As soon as this boat was gone, we had no doubt but that we were abandoned; yet we were not fully convinced of it till the boats had disappeared.

It was now that we had need of all our courage, which, however, forsook us more than once: we really believed that we were sacrificed, and with one accord, we cried that this desertion was premeditated. We all swore to revenge ourselves if we had the good fortune to reach the shore, and there is no doubt but that, if we could have overtaken, the next day, those who had fled in the boats, an obstinate combat would have taken place between them and us.

It was then that some persons who had been marked out for the boats, deeply regretted that they had preferred the raft, because duty and honor had pointed out this post to them. We could mention some persons: for example, Mr. Correard, among others, was to go in one of the boats; but twelve of the workmen, whom we commanded, had been set down for the raft; he thought that in his quality of commander of engineers, it was his duty not to separate from the majority of those who had been confided to him, and who had promised to follow him wherever the exigencies of the service might require; from that moment his fate became inseparable from theirs, and he exerted himself to the utmost to obtain the governor's permission to have his men embarked in the same boat as himself; but seeing that he could obtain nothing to ameliorate the fate of these brave men, he told the governor that he was incapable of committing an act of baseness: that since he would not put his workmen in the same boat with him, he begged him to allow him to go on the raft with them, which was granted.

Several military officers imitated their example; only two of those who were to command the troops did not think fit to place themselves upon the raft, the equipment of which, in truth, could not inspire much confidence.

One of them, Captain Beinière, placed himself in the long-boat with 36 of his soldiers. We had been told that these troops had been charged to superintend the proceedings of the other boats, and to fire upon those who should attempt to abandon the raft. It is true, as we have seen above, that some brave soldiers listening, perhaps, more to the voice of humanity and French honor, than to the strict maxims of discipline, were desirous of employing their arms against those who basely abandoned us, but, that their will and their actions were paralized by the passive obedience which they owed to their officers, who opposed this resolution.

The other, Mr. Danglas, a lieutenant, who had lately left the *gardes-du-corps*, had at first embarked with us upon the raft, where his post was assigned him, but when he saw the danger which he incurred on this unstable machine, he made haste to quit it, on the pretext that he had forgotten something on board the frigate, and did not return. It was he whom we saw, armed with a carbine, threaten to fire on the barge of the governor, when it began to move from the frigate. This movement, and some other actions which were taken for madness, nearly cost him his life; for while he was thus giving himself up to a kind of extravagance, the captain took flight, and abandoned him on board the frigate with the sixty-three men whom he left there. When M. Danglas saw himself treated in this manner, he gave marks of the most furious despair. They were obliged to hinder him from attempting his own life. With loud cries he invoked death, which he believed inevitable in the midst of perils so imminent. It is certain that if Mr. Espiau, who had his long-boat already full, had not returned to take from on board the frigate, the forty-six men, among whom, was Mr. Danglas, he and all his companions would not, perhaps, have experienced a better fate than the seventeen who were finally left on board the Medusa.

After the disappearance of the boats, the consternation was extreme: all the terrors of thirst and famine arose before our imaginations, and we had besides to contend with a perfidious element, which already

covered the half of our bodies: when recovered from their stupefaction, the sailors and soldiers gave themselves up to despair; all saw inevitable destruction before them, and gave vent in lamentations to the gloomy thoughts which agitated them. All we said did not at first avail to calm their fears, in which we however participated, but which a greater degree of strength of mind enabled us to dissemble. At last, a firm countenance and consoling words succeeded in calming them by degrees, but could not wholly dispel the terror with which they were struck; for according to the judicious reflection, made after reading our deplorable story, by Mr. Jay, whose authority we quote with pleasure, " To support extreme misfor-
" tunes, and what is worthy of remark, to
" bear great fatigues, moral energy is
" much more necessary than corporeal
" strength, nay, than the habit of priva-
" tions and hard labour. On this narrow
" theatre where so many sufferings are
" united, where the most cruel extremes
" of hunger and thirst are experienced,

"strong and indefatigable men who have
"been brought up to the most laborious
"professions, sink in succession under the
"weight of the common destiny, while
"men of a weak constitution, and not
"inured to fatigue, find in their minds
"the strength which their bodies want,
"endure with courage unheard-of trials,
"and issue victorious from their struggle
"with the most horrible afflictions. It is
"to the education they have received, to
"the exercise of their intellectual faculties,
"that they owe this astonishing superiori-
"ty and their deliverance." When tranquillity was a little restored, we began to look upon the raft for the charts, the compass and the anchor, which we presumed had been placed there, from what had been said to us at the time we quitted the frigate. These highly necessary articles had not been put upon our machine. The want of a compass in particular, greatly alarmed us, and we uttered cries of rage and vengeance. Mr. Correard then recollected, that he had seen one in the hands of one of the chief workmen under his command, and en-

quired of this man about it: "Yes, yes," said he, "I have it with me." This news transported us with joy, and we thought that our safety depended on this feeble resource. This little compass was about the size of a crown-piece, and far from correct. He who has not been exposed to events, in which his existence was in imminent peril, can form but a faint idea of the value which one then sets upon the most common and simple objects, with what avidity one seizes the slightest means, that are capable of softening the rigour of the fate with which one has to contend. This compass was given to the commander of the raft; but an accident deprived us of it for ever: it fell, and was lost between the pieces of wood which composed our machine: we had kept it only for a few hours; after this loss, we had nothing to guide us but the rising and setting of the sun.

We had all left the frigate without taking any food: hunger began to be severely felt; we mixed our biscuit-paste (which had fallen into the sea) with a little wine, and we distributed it thus prepared: such was our first meal, and the best we had the whole time we were on the raft.

An order, according to numbers, was fixed for the distribution of our miserable provisions. The ration of wine was fixed at three quarters* a day: we shall say no more of the biscuit: the first distribution consumed it entirely. The day passed over pretty quietly: we conversed on the means which we should employ to save ourselves; we spoke of it as a certainty, which animated our courage: and we kept up that of the soldiers, by cherishing the hope of being soon able to revenge ourselves upon those who had so basely abandoned us. This hope of vengeance inspired us all equally, and we uttered a thousand imprecations against those who had left us a prey to so many misfortunes and dangers. The officer who commanded the raft being unable to move, Mr. Savigny took on himself the care

---

* Trois quarts: it is not said of what measure; probably a pint.—T.

of setting up the mast; he caused the pole of one of the frigate's masts to be cut in two; we employed the main-top-gallant sail; the mast was kept up by the rope which had served to tow us, of which we made shrouds and stays: it was fixed on the anterior third of the raft. The sail trimmed very well, but the effect of it was of very little use to us; it served only when the wind came from behind, and to make the raft preserve this direction it was necessary to trim the sail, as if the wind came athwart. We think that the cross position which our raft always retained, may be attributed to the too great length of the pieces of wood which projected on each side.

In the evening, our hearts and our prayers, with the impulse natural to the unfortunate, were directed towards heaven; we invoked it with fervour, and we derived from our prayers the advantage of hoping in our safety: one must have experienced cruel situations, to imagine what a soothing charm, in the midst of misfortune, is afforded by the sublime idea of a God, the protector of the unfortunate. One consoling idea still pleased our imaginations; we presumed that the little division had sailed for the Isle of Arguin, and that after having landed there a part of its people, would return to our assistance: this idea, which we tried to inspire into our soldiers and sailors, checked their clamours. The night came, and our hopes were not yet fulfilled: the wind freshened, the sea rose considerably. What a dreadful night! Nothing but the idea of seeing the boats the next day, gave some consolation to our people, who being most of them unused to the motion of a vessel,* at every shock of the sea, fell upon each other. Mr. Savigny, assisted by some persons, who, in the midst of this disorder, still retained their presence of mind, fastened some ropes to the pieces of the raft: the men took hold of them, and by means of this support, were better able to resist the force of the waves: some were obliged

---

* The original is *n'ayant pas le pié marin*, not having a sailors foot.

to fasten themselves. In the middle of the night the weather was very bad; very heavy waves rolled upon us, and often threw us down with great violence; the cries of the people were mingled with the roaring of the billows; a dreadful sea lifted us every moment from the raft, and threatened to carry us away. This scene was rendered still more awful by the horrors of a very dark night; for some moments we thought that we saw fires at a distance. We had taken the precaution to hang, at the top of the mast, some gun-powder and pistols, with which we had provided ourselves on board the frigate: we made signals by burning a great many charges of powder; we even fired some pistol-shot, but it seems that these fires were only an illusion of the eyesight, or perhaps they were nothing but the dashing of the breakers.

This whole night we contended against death, holding fast by the ropes which were strongly fastened. Rolled by the waves from the back to the front, and from the front to the back, and sometimes precipitated into the sea, suspended between life and death, lamenting our misfortune, certain to perish, yet still struggling for a fragment of existence with the cruel element which threatened to swallow us up. Such was our situation till day-break; every moment were heard the lamentable cries of the soldiers and sailors; they prepared themselves for death; they bid farewell to each other, imploring the protection of Heaven, and addressing fervent prayers to God: all made vows to him, notwithstanding the certainty that they should never be able to fulfil them. Dreadful situation! How is it possible to form an idea of it, which is not below the truth!

About seven o'clock, in the morning, the sea fell a little, the wind blew with less fury; but what a sight presented itself to our view! Ten or twelve unhappy wretches, having their lower extremities entangled in the openings between the pieces of the raft, had not been able to disengage themselves, and had lost their lives; several others had been carried off by the violence of the sea. At the hour of repast we took fresh numbers, in order to leave no break in the series: we missed twenty men: we will not affirm that this number is very exact, for we found that some soldiers, in order to have more than their ration, took two, and even three numbers. We were so many persons crowded together, that it was absolutely impossible to prevent these abuses.

Amidst these horrors, an affecting scene of filial piety forced us to shed tears: two young men raised and recognised, for their father, an unfortunate man who was stretched senseless under the feet of the people; at first, they thought he was dead, and their despair expressed itself by the most affecting lamentations; it was perceived, however, that this almost inanimate body still had breath; we lavished on him all the assistance in our power; he recovered by degrees, and was restored to life and to the prayers of his sons, who held him fast embraced in their arms. While the rights of nature resumed their empire in this affecting episode of our sad adventures, we had soon the afflicting sight of a melancholy contrast. Two young lads, and a baker, did not fear to seek death, by throwing themselves into the sea, after having taken leave of their companions in misfortune. Already the faculties of our men were singularly impaired; some fancied they saw the land; others, vessels which were coming to save us; all announced to us by their cries these fallacious visions.

We deplored the loss of our unhappy companions; we did not presage, at this moment, the still more terrible scene which was to take place the following night; far from that, we enjoyed a degree of satisfaction, so fully were we persuaded that the boats would come to our relief. The day was fine, and the most perfect tranquillity prevailed on our raft. The evening came, and the boats did not appear. Despondency began again to seize all our people, and a mutinous spirit manifested itself by cries of fury; the voice of the officers was wholly disregarded. When the night came, the sky was covered with thick clouds; the wind, which during the day had been rather high, now became furious, and agitated the sea, which, in an instant, grew very rough.

If the preceding night had been terrible, this was still more horrible. Mountains of water covered us every moment, and broke, with violence, in the midst of us; very happily we had the wind behind us, and the fury of the waves was a little checked by the rapidity of our progress; we drove towards the land. From the violence of the sea, the men passed rapidly from the back to the front of the raft, we were obliged to keep in the centre, the most solid part of the raft; those who could not get there, almost all perished. Before and behind the waves dashed with fury, and carried off the men in spite of all their resistance. At the centre, the crowd was such that some poor men were stifled by the weight of their comrades, who fell upon them every moment; the officers kept themselves at the foot of the little mast, obliged, every instant, to avoid the waves, to call to those who surrounded them to go on the one or the other side, for the waves which came upon us, nearly athwart, gave our raft a position almost perpendicular, so that, in order to counterbalance it, we were obliged to run to that side which was raised up by the sea.

The soldiers and sailors, terrified by the presence of an almost inevitable danger, gave themselves up for lost. Firmly believing that they were going to be swallowed up, they resolved to soothe their last moments by drinking till they lost the use of their reason; we had not strength to oppose this disorder; they fell upon a cask which was at the middle of the raft, made a large hole at one end, and with little tin cups which they had brought from on board the frigate, they each took a pretty large quantity, but they were soon obliged to desist, because the sea water entered by the hole which they had made.

The fumes of the wine soon disordered their brains, already affected by the presence of danger and want of food. Thus inflamed, these men, become deaf to the voice of reason, desired to implicate, in one common destruction, their companions in misfortune; they openly expressed their intention to rid themselves of the officers, who they said, wished to oppose their design, and then to destroy the raft by cutting the ropes which united the different parts that composed it. A moment after, they were proceeding to put this plan in execution. One of them advanced to the edge of the raft with a boarding-axe, and began to strike the cords: this was the signal for revolt: we advanced in order to stop these madmen: he who was armed with the axe, with which he even threatened an officer, was the first victim: a blow with a sabre put an end to his existence. This man was an Asiatic, and soldier in a colonial regiment: a colossal stature, short curled hair, an extremely large nose, an enormous mouth, a sallow complexion, gave him a hideous air. He had placed himself, at first, in the middle of the raft, and at every blow of his fist he overthrew those who stood in his way; he inspired the greatest terror, and nobody dared to approach him. If there had been half-a-dozen like him, our destruction would have been inevitable.

Some persons, desirous of prolonging their existence, joined those who wished to preserve the raft, and armed themselves : of this number were some subaltern officers and many passengers. The mutineers drew their sabres, and those who had none, armed themselves with knives: they advanced resolutely against us; we put ourselves on our defence: the attack was going to begin. Animated by despair, one of the mutineers lifted his sabre against an officer; he immediately fell, pierced with wounds. This firmness awed them a moment; but did not at all diminish their rage. They ceased to threaten us, and presenting a front bristling with sabres and bayonets, they retired to the back part, to execute their plan. One of them pretended to rest himself on the little railing which formed the sides of the raft, and with a knife began to cut the cords. Being informed by a servant, we rushed upon him—a soldier attempted to defend him—threatened an officer with his knife, and in attempting to strike him, only pierced his coat— the officer turned round—overpowered his adversary, and threw both him and his comrade into the sea!

After this there were no more partial affairs: the combat became general. Some cried lower the sail; a crowd of madmen instantly threw themselves on the yards and the shrouds, and cut the stays, and let the mast fall, and nearly broke the thigh of a captain of foot, who fell senseless. He was seized by the soldiers, who threw him into the sea: we perceived it—saved him, and placed him on a barrel, from which he was taken by the seditious; who were going to cut out his eyes with a penknife. Exasperated by so many cruelties, we no longer kept any measures, and charged them furiously. With our sabres drawn we traversed the lines which the soldiers formed, and many atoned with their lives for a moment of delusion. Several passengers displayed much courage and coolness in these cruel moments.

Mr. Corréard was fallen into a kind of trance, but hearing every moment cries of " *To arms! To us, comrades! We are undone!*" joined to the cries and imprecations of the wounded and the dying, he was soon roused from his lethargy. The increasing confusion made him sensible that it was necessary to be upon his guard. Armed with his sabre, he assembled some of his workmen on the front of the raft, and forbid them to hurt any one unless they were attacked. He remained almost always with them, and they had several times to defend themselves against the attacks of the mutineers; who falling into the sea, returned by the front of the raft; which placed Mr. Corréard and his little troop between two dangers, and rendered their position very difficult to be defended. Every moment men presented themselves, armed with knives, sabres and bayonets; many had carbines, which they used as clubs. The workmen did their utmost to stop them, by presenting the point of their sabres; and, notwithstanding the repugnance they felt to combat their unhappy countrymen, they were however obliged to use their arms without reserve; because many of the mutineers attacked them with fury, it was necessary to repulse them in the same manner. In this action some of the workmen received large wounds; he who commanded them reckons a great number, which he received in the various combats they had to maintain. At last their united efforts succeeded in dispersing the masses that advanced furiously against them.

During this combat, Mr. Corréard was informed, by one of his workmen who remained faithful, that one of their comrades, named Dominique, had taken part with the mutineers, and that he had just been thrown into the sea. Immediately forgetting the fault and the treachery of this man, he threw himself in after him, at the place where the voice of the wretch had just been heard calling for assistance: he seized him by the hair, and had the good fortune to get him on board. Dominique had received, in a charge, several sabre wounds, one of which had laid open his head. Nothwithstanding the darkness we found the wound, which appeared to us to be very considerable. One of the workmen gave his handkerchief to bind it up and stanch the blood. Our care revived this wretch; but as soon as he recovered his strength, the ungrateful Dominique, again forgetting his duty and the signal service that he had just received from us, went to rejoin the mutineers. So much baseness and fury did not go unpunished; and soon afterwards, while combating us anew, he met with his death, from which he, in fact, did not merit to be rescued, but which he would probably have avoided, if faithful to honor and to gratitude, he had remained among us.

Just when we had almost finished applying a kind of dressing to the wounds of Dominique, another voice was heard; it was that of the unfortunate woman who was on the raft with us, and whom the madmen had thrown into the sea, as well as her husband, who defended her with courage. Mr. Corréard, in despair at seeing two poor wretches perish, whose lamentable cries, especially those of the woman, pierced his heart, seized a large rope which was on the front of the raft, which he fastened round the middle of his body, and threw himself, a second time, into the sea, whence he was so happy as to rescue the woman, who invoked, with all her might, the aid of Our Lady of Laux, while her husband was likewise saved by the chief workman, Lavillette. We seated these two poor people upon dead bodies, with their backs leaning against a barrel. In a few minutes they had recovered their senses. The first thought of the woman was to enquire the name of him who had saved her, and to testify to him the warmest gratitude. Thinking, doubtless, that her words did not sufficiently express her sentiments, she recollected that she had, in her pocket, a little snuff, and immediately offered it to him—it was all she possessed. Touched by this present, but not making use of this antiscorbutic, Mr. Corréard, in turn, made a present of it to a poor sailor, who used it three or four days. But a more affecting scene, which it is impossible for us to describe, is the joy which this unfortunate couple displayed when they had sufficiently recovered their senses to see that they were saved.

The mutineers being repulsed, as we have said above, left us at this moment a little repose. The moon with her sad beams, illumined this fatal raft, this narrow space, in which were united so many heart-rending afflictions, so many cruel distresses, a fury so insensate, a courage so heroic, the most pleasing and generous sentiments of nature and humanity.

The man and his wife, who just before had seen themselves attacked with sabres and bayonets, and thrown at the same moment into the waves of a stormy sea, could hardly believe their senses when they found themselves in each others arms. They felt, they expressed, so fervently, the happiness which they were alas, to enjoy for so short a time, that this affecting sight might have drawn tears from the most insensible heart; but in this terrible moment, when we were but just breathing after the most furious attack, when we were forced to be constantly on our guard, not only against the attacks of the men, but also against the fury of the waves: few of us had time, if we may say so, to suffer ourselves to be moved by this scene of conjugal friendship.

Mr. Corréard, one of those whom it had most agreeably affected, hearing the woman still recommend herself, as she had done when in the sea, to our Lady of Laux, exclaiming every instant, " our good Lady of Laux do not forsake us," recollected that there was, in fact, in the Department of the Upper Alps, a place of devotion so called,* and asked her if she came from that country. She replied in the affirmative, and said she had quitted it 24 years before, and that since that time she had been in the Campaigns in Italy, &c. as a sutler; that she had never quitted our armies. "Therefore," said she, "preserve my life, you see that I am a useful woman." "Oh! if you knew how often I also have braved death on the field of battle, to carry assistance to our brave men." Then she amused herself with giving some account of her campaigns. She mentioned those she had assisted, the provisions which she had provided them, the brandy with which she had treated them. "Whether they had money or not,"

---

* Our Lady of Laux is in the Department of the Upper Alps, not far from Gap. A church has been built there, the patroness of which is much celebrated, in the country, for her miracles. The lame, the gouty, the paralytic, found there relief, which it is said, never failed. Unfortunately, this miraculous power did not extend, it seems, to shipwrecked persons: at least the poor sutler drew but little advantage from it.

said she, " I always let them have my goods. Sometimes a battle made me lose some of my poor debtors; but then, after the victory, others paid me double or triple the value of the provisions which they had consumed before the battle. Thus I had a share in their victory." The idea of owing her life to Frenchmen, at this moment, seemed still to add to her happiness. Unfortunate woman! she did not foresee the dreadful fate that awaited her among us! Let us return to our raft.

After this second check, the fury of the soldiers suddenly abated, and gave place to extreme cowardice: many of them fell at our feet and asked pardon, which was instantly granted them. It is here, the place to observe and to proclaim aloud for the honour of the French army, which has shewn itself as great, as courageous, under reverses, as formidable in battle, that most of these wretches were not worthy to wear its uniform. They were the scum of all countries, the refuse of the prisons, where they had been collected to make up the force charged with the defence and the protection of the colony.

When, for the sake of health, they were made to bathe in the sea, a ceremony from which some of them had the modesty to endeavour to excuse themselves, the whole crew had ocular demonstration that it was not upon the *breast* that these heroes wore the insignia of the exploits, which had led them to serve the state in the Ports of Toulon, Brest or Rochefort.

This is not the moment, and perhaps we are not competent to examine whether the penalty of branding, as it is re-established in our present code, is compatible with the true object of all good legislation, that of correcting while punishing, of striking only as far as is necessary to prevent and preserve; in short, of producing the greatest good to all, with the least possible evil to individuals. Reason at least seems to demonstrate, and what has passed before our own eyes authorises us to believe that it is as dangerous, as inconsistent, to entrust arms for the protection of society, to the hands of those whom society has itself rejected from its bosom; that it implies a contradiction to require courage, generosity, and that devotedness which commands a noble heart to sacrifice itself for its country and fellow creatures, from wretches branded, degraded by corruption, in whom every moral energy is destroyed, or eternally compressed by the weight of the indelible opprobrium which renders them aliens to their country, which separates them for ever from the rest of mankind.

We soon had on board our raft a fresh proof of the impossibility of depending on the permanence of any honorable sentiment in the hearts of beings of this description.

Thinking that order was restored, we had returned to our post at the center of the raft, only we took the precaution to retain our arms. It was nearly midnight: after an hour's apparent tranquillity, the soldiers rose again: their senses were entirely deranged; they rushed upon us like madmen, with their knives or sabres in their hands. As they were in full possession of their bodily strength, and were also armed, we were forced again to put ourselves on our defence. Their revolt was the more dangerous, as in their delirium they were entirely deaf to the cries of reason. They attacked us; we charged them in our turn, and soon the raft was covered with their dead bodies. Those among our adversaries who had no arms, attempted to tear us with their teeth; several of us were cruelly bitten; Mr. Savigny was himself bitten in the legs and the shoulder; he received also a wound with a knife in his right arm, which deprived him, for a long time, of the use of the fourth and little fingers of that hand; many others were wounded; our clothes were pierced in many places by knives and sabres. One of our workmen was also seized by four of the mutineers, who were going to throw him into the sea. One of them had seized him by the right leg, and was biting him cruelly in the sinew above the heel. The others were beating him severely with their sabres and the but end of their carbines; his cries made us fly to his aid. On this occasion, the brave Lavillette, ex-serjeant of the artillery on foot, of the old guard, behaved with courage worthy of the highest praise: we rushed on these desperadoes, after the example of Mr. Corréard, and soon rescued the workman from the danger which threatened him. A few moments after, the mutineers, in another charge, seized on the sub-lieutenant Lozach, whom they took, in their delirium, for Lieutenant Danglas, of whom we have spoken above, and who had abandoned the raft when we were on the point of putting off from the frigate. The soldiers, in general, bore much ill will to this officer, who had seen little service, and whom they reproached with having treated them harshly while they were in garrison in the Isle of Rhé. It would have been a favorable opportunity for them to satiate their rage upon him, and the thirst of vengeance and destruction which animated them to fancy that they had found him in the person of Mr. Lozach, they were going to throw him into the sea. In truth, the soldiers almost equally disliked the latter, who had served only in the Vendean bands of Saint Pol de Leon. We believed this officer lost, when his voice being heard, informed us that it was still possible to save him. Immediately Messrs. Clairet, Savigny, l'Heureux, Lavillette, Coudin, Corréard, and some workmen, having formed themselves into little parties, fell upon the insurgents with so much impetuosity that they overthrew all who opposed them, recovered Mr. Lozach, and brought him back to the center of the raft.

The preservation of this officer cost us infinite trouble. Every moment the soldiers demanded that he should be given up to them, always calling him by the name of Danglas. It was in vain we attempted to make them sensible of their mistake, and to recal to their memory, that he, whom they demanded, had returned on board the frigate, as they had themselves seen; their cries drowned the voice of reason; every thing was in their eyes Danglas; they saw him every where, they furiously and unceasingly demanded his head, and it was only by force of arms, that we succeeded in repressing their rage, and in silencing their frightful cries.

On this occasion we had also reason to be alarmed for the safety of Mr. Coudin. Wounded and fatigued by the attacks which we had sustained with the disaffected, and in which he had displayed the most dauntless courage, he was reposing on a barrel, holding in his arms a sailor boy, of twelve years of age, to whom he had attached himself. The mutineers seized him with his barrel, and threw him into the sea with the boy, whom he still held fast; notwithstanding this burden, he had the presence of mind to catch hold of the raft, and to save himself from this extreme danger. Dreadful night! thy gloomy veil covered these cruel combats, instigated by the most terrible despair.

We cannot conceive how a handful of individuals could resist such a considerable number of madmen. There were, certainly, not more than twenty of us to resist all these furious wretches. Let it, however, not be imagined, that we preserved our reason unimpaired amidst all this disorder; terror, alarm, the most cruel privations had greatly affected our intellectual faculties; but being a little less deranged than the unfortunate soldiers, we energetically opposed their determination to cut the cords of the raft. Let us be allowed to make some reflections on the various sensations with which we were affected.

The very first day, Mr. Griffon lost his senses so entirely, that he threw himself into the sea, intending to drown himself. Mr. Savigny saved him with his own hand. His discourse was vague and unconnected. He threw himself into the water a second time, but by a kind of instinct he kept hold of one of the cross pieces of the raft: and was again rescued.

The following is an account of what Mr. Savigny experienced in the beginning of the night. His eyes closed in spite of himself, and he felt a general lethargy; in this situation the most agreeable images played before his fancy; he saw around him, a country covered with fine plantations, and he found himself in the presence of objects which delighted all his senses; yet he reasoned on his situation, and felt that courage alone would recover him from this species of trance; he asked the master gunner of the frigate for some wine: who procured him a little; and he recovered in a degree from this state of torpor. If the unfortunate men, when they were attacked by these first symptoms, had not had resolution to struggle against them, their death was certain. Some became furious; others threw themselves into the sea, taking leave of their comrades with great coolness; some said " Fear nothing, I am going to fetch you assistance : in a short time you will see me again." In the midst of this general madness, some unfortunate wretches were seen to rush upon their comrades with their sabres drawn, demanding the *wing of a chicken*, or *bread* to appease the hunger which devoured them; others called for their hammocks, " *to go*," they said, " *between the decks of the frigate and take some moments' repose.*" Many fancied themselves still on board the Medusa, surrounded with the same objects which they saw there every day. Some saw ships, and called them to their assistance, or a harbour, in the back ground of which there was a magnificent city.

Mr. Corréard fancied he was travelling through the fine plains of Italy; one of the officers said to him, gravely, " *I remember that we have been deserted by the boats; but fear nothing; I have just written to the governor, and in a few hours we shall be saved.*" Mr. Corréard replied in the same tone, and as if he had been in an ordinary situation, " *Have you a pigeon to carry your orders with as much celerity?*" The cries and the tumult soon roused us from the state in which we were plunged; but scarcely was tranquillity restored, when we sunk back into the same species of trance: so that the next day we seemed to awake from a painful dream, and asked our companions if, during their sleep, they had seen combats and heard cries of despair. Some of them replied that they had been continually disturbed by the same visions, and that they were exhausted with fatigue: all thought themselves deceived by the illusions of a frightful dream.

When we recal to our minds those terrible scenes, they present themselves to our imagination like those frightful dreams which sometimes make a profound impression on us; so that, when we awake, we remember the different circumstances which rendered our sleep so agitated. All these horrible events, from which we have escaped by a miracle, appear to us like a point in our existence: we compare them with the fits of a burning fever, which has been accompanied by a delirium: a thousand objects appear before the imagination of the patient: when restored to health, he sometimes recollects the visions that have tormented him during the fever which consumed him, and exalted his imagination. We were really seized with a fever on the brain, the consequence of a mental exaltation carried to the extreme. As soon as daylight beamed upon us, we were much more calm: darkness brought with it a renewal of the disorder in our weakened intellects. We observed in ourselves that the natural terror, inspired by the cruel situation in which we were, greatly increased in the silence of the night: then all objects seemed to us much more terrible.

After these different combats, worn out with fatigue, want of food and of sleep, we endeavoured to take a few moments' repose, at length daylight came, and disclosed all the horrors of the scene. A great number had, in their delirium, thrown themselves into the sea: we found that between sixty and sixty-five men had perished during the night; we calculated that, at least, a fourth part had drowned themselves in despair. We had lost only two on our side, neither of whom was an officer. The deepest despondency was painted on every face;

every one, now that he was come to himself, was sensible of his situation; some of us, shedding tears of despair, bitterly deplored the rigour of our fate.

We soon discovered a new misfortune; the rebels, during the tumult, had thrown into the sea two barrels of wine, and the only two casks of water that we had on the raft.* As soon as Mr. Corréard perceived that they were going to throw the wine into the sea, and that the barrels were almost entirely made loose, he resolved to place himself on one of them; where he was continually thrown to and fro by the impulse of the waves; but he did not let go his hold. His example was followed by some others, who seized the second cask, and remained some hours at that dangerous post, After much trouble they had succeeded in saving these two casks; which being every

---

* One of the water casks was recovered; but the mutineers had made a large hole in it, and the sea water got in, so that the fresh water was quite spoiled; we, however, kept the little cask as well as one of the wine barrels, which was empty. These two casks were afterwards of use to us.

moment violently driven against their legs had bruised them severely. Being unable to hold out any longer, they made some representations to those who, with Mr. Savigny, employed all their efforts to maintain order and preserve the raft. One of them took his (Mr. Corréard) place; others relieved the rest: but finding this service too difficult, and being assaulted by the mutineers, they forsook this post. Then the barrels were thrown into the sea.

Two casks of wine had been consumed the preceding day; we had only one left, and we were above sixty in number; so that it was necessary to put ourselves on half allowance.

At daybreak the sea grew calm, which enabled us to put up our mast again; we then did our utmost to direct our course towards the coast. Whether it were an illusion or reality we thought we saw it, and that we distinguished the burning air of the Zaara Desert. It is, in fact, very probable that we were not very distant from it, for we had had winds from the sea which had blown violently. In the sequel we spread the sail indifferently to every wind that blew, so that one day we approached the coast, on the next ran into the open sea.

As soon as our mast was replaced, we made a distribution of wine; the unhappy soldiers murmured and accused us for privations, which we bore as well as they: they fell down with fatigue. For forty-eight hours we had taken nothing, and had been obliged to struggle incessantly against a stormy sea; like them we could hardly support ourselves; courage alone still made us act. We resolved to employ all possible means to procure fish. We collected all the tags from the soldiers, and made little hooks of them; we bent a bayonet to catch sharks: all this availed us nothing; the currents carried our hooks under the raft, where they got entangled. A shark bit at the bayonet, and straightened it. We gave up our project. But an extreme resource was necessary to preserve our wretched existence. We tremble with horror at being obliged to mention that which we made use of! we feel our pen drop from our hand; a deathlike chill pervades all our limbs; our hair stands erect on our heads!—Reader, we beseech you, do not feel indignation towards men who are already too unfortunate; but have compassion on them, and shed some tears of pity on their unhappy fate.

Those whom death had spared in the disastrous night which we have just described, fell upon the dead bodies with which the raft was covered, and cut off pieces, which some instantly devoured. Many did not touch them; almost all the officers were of this number. Seeing that this horrid nourishment had given strength to those who had made use of it, it was proposed to dry it, in order to render it a little less disgusting. Those who had firmness enough to abstain from it took a larger quantity of wine. We tried to eat swordbelts and cartouch-boxes. We succeeded in swallowing some little morsels. Some eat linen. Others pieces of leather from the hats, on which there was a little grease, or rather dirt. We were obliged to give up these last means. A sailor attempted to eat excrements, but he could not succeed.

The day was calm and fine: a ray of hope allayed our uneasiness for a moment. We still expected to see the boats or some vessels; we addressed our prayers to the Eternal, and placed our confidence in him. The half of our men were very weak, and bore on all their features the stamp of approaching dissolution. The evening passed over, and no assistance came. The darkness of this third night increased our alarm; but the wind was slight, and the sea less agitated. We took some moment's repose: a repose which was still more terrible than our situation the preceding day; cruel dreams added to the horrors of our situation. Tormented by hunger and thirst, our plaintive cries sometimes awakened from his sleep, the wretch who was reposing close to us. We were even now up to our knees in the water, so that we could only repose standing, pressed against each other to form a solid mass. The fourth morning's sun, after our departure, at length rose on our disaster, and shewed us ten or twelve of our companions extended lifeless on the raft. This sight affected us the more as it announced to us that our bodies, deprived of existence, would soon be stretched on the same place. We gave their bodies to the sea for a grave; reserving only one, destined to feed those who, the day before, had clasped his trembling hands, vowing him an eternal friendship. This day was fine; our minds, longing for more agreeable sensations, were harmonized by the soothing aspect of nature, and admitted a ray of hope. About four in the afternoon a circumstance occurred which afforded us some consolation: a shoal of flying fish passed under the raft, and as the extremities left an infinite number of vacancies between the pieces which composed it, the fish got entangled in great numbers. We threw ourselves upon them, and caught a considerable quantity: we took near two hundred and put them in an empty cask;* as we caught them we opened them to take out what is called the milt. This food seemed delicious to us; but one man would have wanted a thousand. Our first impulse was to address new thanksgivings to God for this unexpected benefit.

An ounce of gunpowder had been found in the morning, and dried in the sun, during the day, which was very fine; a steel,

---

* These fish are very small; the largest is not equal to a small herring.

some gun-flints and tinder were also found in the same parcel. After infinite trouble we succeeded in setting fire to some pieces of dry linen. We made a large hole in one side of an empty cask, and placed at the bottom of it several things which we wetted, and on this kind of scaffolding we made our fire: we placed it on a barrel that the sea-water might not put out our fire. We dressed some fish, which we devoured with extreme avidity; but our hunger was so great and our portion of fish so small, that we added to it some human flesh, which dressing rendered less disgusting; it was this which the officers touched, for the first time. From this day we continued to use it; but we could not dress it any more, as we were entirely deprived of the means; our barrel catching fire we extinguished it without being able to save any thing whereby to light it again next day. The powder and the tinder were entirely consumed. This repast gave us all fresh strength to bear new fatigues. The night was tolerable, and would have appeared happy had it not been signalised by a new massacre.

Some Spaniards, Italians, and Negroes,

who had remained neuter in the first mutiny, and some of whom had even ranged themselves on our side,* formed a plot to throw us all into the sea, hoping to execute their design by falling on us by surprise. These wretches suffered themselves to be persuaded by the negroes, who assured them that the coast was extremely near, and promised, that when they were once on shore, they would enable them to traverse Africa without danger. The desire of saving themselves, or perhaps the wish to seize on the money and valuables, which had been put into a bag, hung to the mast,† had inflamed the imagination of these unfortunate wretches. We were obliged to take our

---

* This plot, as we learned afterwards, was formed particularly by a Piedmontese serjeant; who, for two days past, had endeavoured to insinuate himself with us, in order to gain our confidence. The care of the wine was entrusted to him: he stole it in the night, and distributed it to some of his friends.

† We had all put together in one bag the money we had, in order to purchase provisions and hire camels to carry the sick, in case we should land on the edge of the desert. The sum was fifteen hundred francs. Fifteen of us were saved, and each had a hundred francs. The commander of the raft and a captain of infantry divided it.

arms again; but how were we to discover the guilty? they were pointed out to us, by our sailors, who remained faithful, and ranged themselves near us; one of them had refused to engage in the plot. The first signal, for combat, was given by a Spaniard, who, placing himself behind the mast, laid fast hold of it, made the sign of the Cross with one hand, invoking the name of God, and held a knife in the other: the sailors seized him, and threw him into the sea. The servant of an officer of the troops on board was in the plot. He was an Italian from the light artillery of the Ex-King of his country. When he perceived that the plot was discovered, he armed himself with the last boarding-axe that there was on the raft, wrapped himself in a piece of drapery, which he wore folded over his breast, and, of his own accord, threw himself into the sea. The mutineers rushed forward to avenge their comrades, a terrible combat again ensued, and both sides fought with desperate fury. Soon the fatal raft was covered with dead bodies, and flowing with blood which ought to have been shed in another cause, and by other hands. In this tumult cries, with which we were familiar, were renewed, and we heard the imprecations of the horrid rage which demanded the head of Lieutenant Danglas! Our readers know that we could not satisfy this mad rage, because the victim, demanded, had fled the dangers to which we were exposed; but even if this officer had remained among us, we should most certainly have defended his life at the expence of our own, as we did that of Lieutenant Lozach. But it was not for him that we were reduced to exert, against these madmen, all the courage we possessed.

We again replied to the cries of the assailants, that he whom they demanded was not with us; but we had no more success in persuading them; nothing could make them recollect themselves; we were obliged to continue to combat them, and to oppose force to those over whom reason had lost all its influence. In this confusion the unfortunate woman was, a second time, thrown into the sea. We perceived it, and Mr. Coudin, assisted by some workmen, took her up again, to prolong, for a few moments, her torments and her existence.

In this horrible night, Lavillette gave further proofs of the rarest intrepidity. It was to him, and to some of those who have escaped the consequences of our misfortunes, that we are indebted for our safety. At length, after unheard-of efforts, the mutineers were again repulsed, and tranquillity restored. After we had escaped this new danger, we endeavoured to take some moment's repose. The day at length rose on us for the fifth time. We were now only thirty left; we had lost four or five of our faithful sailors; those who survived were in the most deplorable state; the sea-water had almost entirely excoriated our lower extremities; we were covered with contusions or wounds, which, irritated by the salt-water, made us utter every moment piercing cries; so that there were not above twenty of us who were able to stand upright or walk. Almost our whole stock was exhausted; we had no more wine than was sufficient for four days, and we had not above a dozen fish left. In four days, said we, we shall be in want of every thing, and death will be unavoidable. Thus arrived the seventh day since we had been abandoned;

we calculated that, in case the boats had not stranded on the coast, they would want, at least, three or four times twenty-four hours to reach St. Louis. Time was further required to equip ships, and for these ships to find us; we resolved to hold out as long as possible. In the course of the day, two soldiers slipped behind the only barrel of wine we had left; they had bored a hole in it, and were drinking by means of a reed; we had all sworn, that he who should employ such means should be punished with death. This law was instantly put in execution, and the two trespassers were thrown into the sea.*

This same day terminated the existence of a child, twelve years of age, named Léon; he died away like a lamp which ceases to burn for want of aliment. Every thing spoke in favor of this amiable young creature, who merited a better fate. His angelic countenance, his melodious voice, the interest inspired by his youth, which was increased by the courage he had shown,

---

* One of these soldiers was the same Piedmontese serjeant of whom we have spoken above; he put his comrades forward, and kept himself concealed in case their plot should fail.

and the services he had performed, for he had already made, in the preceding year, a campaign in the East Indies, all this filled us with the tenderest interest for this young victim, devoted to a death so dreadful and premature. Our old soldiers, and our people in general, bestowed upon him all the care which they thought calculated to prolong his existence. It was in vain; his strength, at last, forsook him. Neither the wine, which we gave him without regret, nor all the means which could be employed, could rescue him from his sad fate; he expired in the arms of Mr. Coudin, who had not ceased to shew him the kindest attention. As long as the strength of this young marine had allowed him to move, he ran continually from one side to the other, calling, with loud cries, for his unhappy mother, water, and food. He walked, without discrimination, over the feet and legs of his companions in misfortune, who, in their turn, uttered cries of anguish, which were every moment repeated. But their complaints were very seldom accompanied by menaces; they pardoned every thing in the poor youth, who had caused them. Besides, he was, in fact, in a state of mental derangement, and in his uninterrupted alienation he could not be expected to behave, as if he had still retained some use of reason.

We were now only twenty-seven remaining; of this number but fifteen seemed likely to live some days: all the rest, covered with large wounds, had almost entirely lost their reason; yet they had a share in the distribution of provisions, and might, before their death, consume thirty or forty bottles of wine, which were of inestimable value to us. We deliberated thus: to put the sick on half allowance would have been killing them by inches. So after a debate, at which the most dreadful despair presided, it was resolved to throw them into the sea. This measure, however repugnant it was to ourselves, procured the survivors wine for six days; when the decision was made, who would dare to execute it? The habit of seeing death ready to pounce upon us as his prey, the certainty of our infallible destruction, without this fatal expedient, every thing in a word, had hardened our hearts, and rendered them callous to all feeling except that of self preservation. Three sailors and a soldier took on themselves this cruel execution: we turned our faces aside, and wept tears of blood over the fate of these unhappy men. Among them were the unfortunate woman and her husband. Both of them had been severely wounded in the various combats: the woman had a thigh broken between the pieces of wood composing the raft, and her husband had received a deep wound with a sabre on his head. Every thing announced their speedy dissolution. We must seek to console ourselves, by the belief, that our cruel resolution shortened, but for a few moments only, the measure of their existence.

This French woman, to whom soldiers and Frenchmen gave the sea for a tomb, had partaken for twenty years in the glorious fatigues of our armies; for twenty years she had afforded to the brave, on the field of battle, either the assistance which they needed, or soothing consolations...It is in the midst of her friends; it is by the hands of her friends...Readers, who shudder at the cry of outraged humanity, recollect at least, that it was other men, fellow countrymen, comrades, who had placed us in this horrible situation.

This dreadful expedient saved the fifteen who remained; for, when we were found by the Argus, we had very little wine left, and it was the sixth day after the cruel sacrifice which we have just described: the victims, we repeat it, had not above forty-eight hours to live, and by keeping them on the raft, we should absolutely have been destitute of the means of existence two days before we were found. Weak as we were, we considered it as certain that it would have been impossible for us to hold out, even twenty-four hours, without taking some food. After this catastrophe, which inspired us with a degree of horror not to be overcome, we threw the arms into the sea; we reserved, however, one sabre in case it should be wanted to cut a rope or piece of wood.

After all this, we had scarcely sufficient food on the raft, to last for the six days, and they were the most wretched immaginable. Our dispositions had become soured: even in sleep, we figured to ourselves the sad end of all our unhappy companions, and we loudly invoked death.

A new event, for every thing was an *event* for wretches for whom the universe was reduced to a flooring of a few toises in extent, who were the sport of the winds and waves, as they hung suspended over the abyss; an event then happened which happily diverted our attention from the horrors of our situation. All at once a white butterfly, of the species so common in France, appeared fluttering over our heads, and settled on our sail. The first idea which, as it were, inspired each of us made us consider this little animal as the harbinger, which brought us the news of a speedy approach to land, and we snatched at this hope with a kind of delirium of joy. But it was the ninth day that we passed upon the raft; the torments of hunger consumed our entrails; already some of the soldiers and sailors devoured, with haggard eyes, this wretched prey, and seemed ready to dispute it with each other. Others considered this butterfly as a messenger of heaven, declared that they took the poor insect under their protection, and hindered any injury being done to it. We turned our wishes and our eyes towards the land, which we so ardently longed for, and which we every moment fancied we saw rise before us. It is certain that we could not be far from it: for the butterflies continued, on the following days, to come and flutter about our sail, and the same day we had another sign equally positive: for we saw a *(goeland)* flying over our raft. This second visitor did not allow us to doubt of our being very near to the African shore, and we persuaded ourselves that we should soon be thrown upon the coast by the force of the currents. How often did we then, and in the following days, invoke a tempest to throw us on the coast, which, it seemed to us, we were on the point of touching.

The hope which had just penetrated the inmost recesses of our souls, revived our enfeebled strength, and inspired us with an ardour, an activity, of which we should not have thought ourselves capable. We again had recourse to all the means which we had before employed, to catch fish. Above all, we eagerly longed for the (goeland), which appeared several times tempted to settle on the end of our machine. The impatience of our desire increased, when we saw several of its companions join it, and keep following us till our deliverance; but all attempts to draw them to us were in vain; not one of them suffered itself to be taken by the snares we had laid for them. Thus our destiny, on the fatal raft, was to be incessantly tossed between transitory illusions and continued torments, and we never experienced an agreeable sensation without being, in a manner, condemned to atone for it, by the anguish of some new suffering, by the irritating pangs of hope always deceived.

Another care employed us this day: as soon as we were reduced to a small number, we collected the little strength we had remaining; we loosened some planks on the front of the raft, and with some pretty long pieces of wood, raised in the center a kind of platform, on which we reposed: all the effects which we had been able to collect, were placed upon it, and served to render it less hard; besides, they hindered the sea from passing with so much facility through the intervals between the different pieces of the raft; but the waves came across, and sometimes covered us entirely.

It was on this new theatre that we re-

solved to await death in a manner worthy of Frenchmen, and with perfect resignation. The most adroit among us, to divert our thoughts, and to make the time pass with more rapidity, got their comrades to relate to us their passed triumphs, and sometimes, to draw comparisons between the hardships they had undergone in their glorious campaigns, and the distresses we endured upon our raft. The following is what Lavillette the serjeant of artillery told us: " I have
" experienced, in my various naval cam-
" paigns, all the fatigues, all the privations
" and all the dangers, which it is possible
" to meet with at sea, but none of my
" past sufferings, is comparable to the
" extreme pain and privations which I
" endure here. In my last campaigns in
" 1813 and 1814, in Germany and France,
" I shared all the fatigues which were al-
" ternately caused us by victory and retreat.
" I was at the glorious days of Lutzen,
" Bautzen, Dresden, Leipzig, Hanau, Mont-
" mirail, Champaubert, Montereau," &c.
" Yes," continued he, " all that I suf-
" fered in so many forced marches, and in
" the midst of the privations which were

" the consequences of them, was nothing in
" comparison with what I endure on this
" frightful machine. In those days, when
" the French valour shewed itself in all
" its lustre, and always worthy of a free
" people, I had hardly anything to fear,
" but during the battle; but here, I often
" have the same dangers, and what is more
" dreadful, I have to combat Frenchmen
" and comrades. I have to contend, be-
" sides, with hunger and thirst, with a tem-
" pestuous sea, full of dangerous monsters,
" and with the ardour of a burning sun,
" which is not the least of our enemies. Co-
" vered with ancient scars and fresh wounds,
" which I have no means of dressing, it is
" physically impossible for me to save my-
" self from this extreme danger, if it should
" be prolonged for a few days."

The sad remembrance of the critical situation of our country also mingled with our grief; and certainly, of all the afflictions we experienced, this was not the least, to us, who had almost all of us left it, only that we might no longer be witnesses of the hard laws, of the afflicting dependence, under which, it is bowed down by enemies jealous of our glory and of our power. These thoughts, we do not fear to say so, and to boast of it, afflicted us still more than the inevitable death which we were almost certain of meeting on our raft. Several of us regretted not having fallen in the defence of France. At least, said they, if it had been possible for us to measure our strength once more, with the enemies of our independence, and our liberty! Others found some consolation in the death which awaited us, because we should no longer have to groan under the shameful yoke which oppresses the country. Thus passed the last days of our abode on the raft. Our time was almost wholly employed in speaking of our unhappy country: all our wishes, our last prayers were for the happiness of France.

During the first days and nights of our being abandoned, the weather was very cold, but we bore the immersion pretty well; and during the last nights that we passed on the raft, every time that a wave rolled over us, it produced a very disagreeable sensation, and made us utter plaintive cries, so that each of us employed means to avoid it: some raised their heads, by means of pieces of wood, and made with whatever they could find a kind of parapet, against which the wave broke: others sheltered themselves behind empty casks which were placed across, along side each other; but these means often proved insufficient; it was only when the sea was very calm that it did not break over us.

A raging thirst, which was redoubled in the daytime by the beams of a burning sun, consumed us: it was such, that we eagerly moistened our parched lips with urine, which we cooled in little tin cups. We put the cup in a place where there was a little water, that the urine might cool the sooner; it often happened that these cups were stolen from those who had thus prepared them. The cup was returned, indeed, to him to whom it belonged, but not till the liquid which it contained was drank. Mr. Savigny observed that the urine of som of us was more agreeable than that of others. There was a passenger who could never prevail on himself to swallow it: in reality, it had not a disagreeable taste; but in some of us it became thick, and extraordinarily acrid: it produced an effect truly worthy of remark: namely, that it was scarcely swallowed, when it excited an inclination to urine anew. We also tried to quench our thirst by drinking sea-water. Mr. Griffon, the governor's secretary, used it continually, he drank ten or twelve glasses in succession. But all these means only diminished our thirst to render it more severe a moment afterwards.

An officer of the army, found by chance, a little lemon, and it may be imagined how valuable this fruit must be to him; he, in fact, reserved it entirely for himself; his comrades, notwithstanding the most pressing entreaties, could not obtain any of it; already emotions of rage were rising in every heart, and if he had not partly yielded to those who surrounded him, they would certainly have taken it from him by force, and he would have perished, the victim of his selfishness. We also disputed for about thirty cloves of garlic, which had been found accidentally in a little bag: all these disputes were generally accompanied with violent threats, and if they had been protracted we should, perhaps, have come to the last extremities.

We had found, also, two little phials which contained a spirituous liquor to clean the teeth; he who possessed them, kept them carefully, and made many difficulties to give one or two drops of this liquid in the hollow of the hand. This liquor, which we believe was an essence of guiacum, cinnamon, cloves, and other aromatic substances, produced on our tongues a delightful sensation, and removed for a few moments the thirst which consumed us. Some of us found pieces of pewter, which, being put into the mouth produced a kind of coolness.

One of the means generally employed, was to put some sea-water into a hat, with which we washed our faces for some time, recurring to it at intervals; we also moistened our hair with it, and held our hands plunged in the water.* Misfortune rendered us ingenious, and every one thought of a thousand means to alleviate his sufferings; extenuated by the most cruel privations, the smallest agreeable sensation was to us a

---

* Persons shipwrecked, in a situation similar to ours, have found great relief by dipping their clothes in the sea, and wearing them thus impregnated with the water; this measure was not employed on the fatal raft.

supreme happiness; thus we eagerly sought a little empty phial, which one of us possessed, and which had formerly contained essence of roses: as soon as we could get hold of it we inhaled, with delight, the perfume which issued from it, and which communicated to our senses the most soothing impressions. Some of us reserved our portion of wine in little tin cups, and sucked up the wine with a quill; this manner of taking it was very beneficial to us, and quenched our thirst much more than if we had drunk it off at once. Even the smell of this liquor was extremely agreeable to us. Mr. Savigny observed that many of us, after having taken their small portion, fell into a state approaching to intoxication, and that there was always more discord among us after the distribution had been made.

The following is one instance, among many, which we could adduce. The tenth day of our being on the raft, after a distribution of wine, Messrs. Clairet, Coudin, Charlot, and one or two of our sailors, conceived the strange idea of destroying themselves, first intoxicating themselves with what remained in our barrel. In vain

Captain Dupont, seconded by Messrs. Lavillette, Savigny, Lheureux, and all the others, opposed their purpose by urgent remonstrances, and by all the firmness of which they were capable—their disordered brains persisted in the mad idea which governed them, and a new combat was on the point of commencing; however, after infinite trouble, we were beginning to bring back Messrs. Clairet and Coudin to the use of their reason; or rather he who watched over us dispelled this fatal quarrel, by turning our attention to the new danger which threatened us, at the moment when cruel discord was, perhaps, about to break out among wretches already a prey to so many other evils—it was a number of sharks which came and surrounded our raft. They approached so near, that we were able to strike them with our sabre, but we could not subdue one of them, notwithstanding the goodness of the weapon we possessed, and the ardour with which the brave Lavillette made use of it. The blows which he struck these monsters, made them replunge into the sea; but a few seconds after, they re-appeared upon the surface, and did not seem at all alarmed at our presence. Their backs rose about 30 centimetres above the water: several of them appeared to us to be at least 10 metres in length.

Three days passed in inexpressible anguish; we despised life to such a degree that many of us did not fear to bathe in sight of the sharks which surrounded our raft; others placed themselves naked on the front part of our machine which was still submerged: these means diminished, a little, their burning thirst. A kind of polypus (mollusques),* known by seamen under the name of *galère*, was frequently driven in great numbers on our raft, and when their long arms clung to our naked bodies, they caused us the most cruel sufferings. Will it be believed, that amidst these dreadful scenes, struggling with inevitable death, some of us indulged in pleasantries which excited a smile, notwithstanding the horror of our situation? One, among others said, joking, "*If the brig is sent to look for us, let us pray to God that she may have the eyes of Argus,*" alluding to the name of

---

* Perhaps a kind of sea-nettle is here meant.

the vessel, which we presumed would be sent after us. This consolatory idea did not quit us an instant, and we spoke of it frequently.

During the day of the 16th, reckoning ourselves to be very near land, eight of the most determined of us, resolved to try to reach the coast: we unfastened a strong fish of a mast,* which made part of the little parapet of which we have spoken, we fixed boards to it at intervals, transversely, by means of great nails, to hinder it from upsetting; a little mast and sail were fixed in the front; we intended to provide ourselves with oars made of barrel staves, cut out with the only sabre we had remaining: we cut pieces of rope, we split them, and made smaller ropes, that were more easy to manage: a hammock cloth, which was by chance on the raft, served for a sail; the dimensions of which, might be about 130 centimetres in breadth and 160 in length: the transverse diameter of the fish was 60 or 70 centimetres, and its length about 12 metres. A certain portion of wine was

---
* What is called a fish, is a long piece of wood concave on one side, serving to be applied to the side of a

assigned to us, and our departure fixed for the next day, the 17th. When our machine was finished, it remained to make a trial of it: a sailor wanting to pass from the front to the back of it, finding the mast in his way, set his foot on one of the cross boards; the weight of his body made it upset, and this accident proved to us the temerity of our enterprise. It was then resolved that we should all await death in our present situation; the cable which fastened the machine to our raft, was made loose, and it drifted away. It is very certain that if we had ventured upon this second raft, weak as we were, we should not have been able to hold out six hours, with our legs in the water, and thus obliged continually to row.

Mean time the night came, and its gloomy shades revived in our minds the most afflicting thoughts; we were convinced that there were not above twelve or fifteen bottles of wine left in our barrel. We began to feel an invincible disgust at the flesh which had till then, scarcely supported us; and we may say that the sight of it inspired

---

mast, to strengthen it when in danger of breaking, it is fastened by strong ropes; hence, to fish a mast.

us with a sentiment of terror, which was doubtless produced by the idea of approaching destruction.

On the 17th, in the morning, the sun appeared entirely free from clouds; after having put up our prayers to the Almighty, we divided among us, a part of our wine; every one was taking with delight his small portion, when a captain of infantry looking towards the horizon, descried a ship, and announced it to us by an exclamation of joy: we perceived that it was a brig; but it was at a very great distance; we could distinguish only the tops of the masts. The sight of this vessel excited in us a transport of joy which it would be difficult to describe; each of us believed his deliverance certain, and we gave a thousand thanks to God; yet, fears mingled with our hopes: we straitened some hoops of casks, to the end of which we tied handkerchiefs of different colours. A man, assisted by us all together, mounted to the top of the mast and waved these little flags.

For above half an hour, we were suspended between hope and fear; some thought they saw the ship become larger, and others affirmed that its course carried it from us: these latter were the only ones whose eyes were not fascinated by hope, for the brig disappeared. From the delirium of joy, we fell into profound despondency and grief; we envied the fate of those whom we had seen perish at our side, and we said to ourselves, when we shall be destitute of every thing, and our strength begins to forsake us, we will wrap ourselves up as well as we can, we will lay ourselves down on this platform, the scene of so many sufferings, and there we will await death with resignation. At last, to calm our despair, we wished to seek some consolation in the arms of sleep; the day before we had been consumed by the fire of a burning sun; this day, to avoid the fierceness of his beams, we made a tent with the sails of the frigate: as soon as it was put up, we all lay down under it, so that we could not perceive what was passing around us. We then proposed to inscribe upon a board an account of our adventures, to write all our names at the bottom of the narrative, and to fasten it to the upper part of the mast, in the hope that it would reach the government and our families.

After we had passed two hours, absorbed in the most cruel reflections, the master gunner of the frigate wishing to go to the front of the raft, went out of our tent; scarcely had he put his head out, when he turned towards us, uttering a loud cry; joy was painted on his countenance, his hands were stretched towards the sea, he scarcely breathed: all that he could say, was, "*Saved! see the brig close upon us.*" And in fact, it was, at the most, half a league distant, carrying a press of sail, and steering so as to come extremely close to us; we precipitately left the tent: even those whom enormous wounds, in the lower extremities, had confined for some days past, always to lie down, crawled to the back part of the raft, to enjoy the sight of this vessel, which was coming to deliver us from certain death. We all embraced each other with transports that looked like delirium, and tears of joy rolled down our cheeks, shrunk by the most cruel privations. Every one seized handkerchiefs, or pieces of linen to make signals to the brig, which was approaching rapidly. Others prostrating themselves, fervently thanked Providence for our miraculous preservation. Our joy redoubled when we perceived a great white flag at the foremast head, and we exclaimed " It is then to French-" men that we shall owe our deliverance." We almost immediately recognised the brig to be the Argus: it was then within two musket shot: we were extremely impatient to see her clue up her sails; she lowered them at length, and fresh cries of joy rose from our raft. The Argus came and lay-to on our starboard, within half a pistol shot. The crew, ranged on the deck and in the shrouds, shewed, by waving their hats and handkerchiefs, the pleasure they felt at coming to the assistance of their unhappy countrymen. A boat was immediately hoisted out; an officer belonging to the brig, whose name was Mr. Lemaigre, had embarked in it, in order to have the pleasure of taking us himself from this fatal machine. This officer, full of humanity and zeal, acquitted himself of his mission in the kindest manner, and took himself, those that were the weakest, to convey them into the boat. After all the others were placed in it, Mr. Lemaigre came and took in his arms Mr. Corréard, whose health was the worst, and who was the most excoriated: he placed him at his side in the boat, bestowed on him all imaginable cares, and spoke to him in the most consoling terms.

In a short time we were all removed on board the Argus, where we met with the lieutenant of the frigate, and some others of those who had been shipwrecked. Pity was painted on every face, and compassion drew tears from all who cast their eyes on us.

Let the reader imagine fifteen unfortunate men, almost naked; their bodies and faces disfigured by the scorching beams of the sun; ten of the fifteen were hardly able to move; our limbs were excoriated, our sufferings were deeply imprinted on our features, our eyes were hollow, and almost wild, and our long beards rendered our appearance still more frightful; we were but the shadows of ourselves. We found on board the brig some very good broth, which had been got ready; as soon as they perceived us, they added some excellent wine to it; thus they restored our almost exhausted strength; they bestowed on us the most generous care and attention; our wounds were dressed, and the next day several of our sick began to recover; however, some of us had a great deal to suffer; for they were placed between decks, very near the kitchen, which augmented the almost insupportable heat of these countries; the want of room in a small vessel, was the cause of this inconvenience. The number of the shipwrecked was indeed too great. Those who did not belong to the marine, were laid upon cables, wrapped in some flags, and placed under the kitchen fire, which exposed them to perish in the night; fire having broken out between decks, about ten o'clock, which had like to have reduced the vessel to ashes; but timely assistance was afforded, and we were saved for the second time. We had scarcely escaped when some of us again become delirious: an officer of the army wanted to throw himself into the sea, to go and look for his pocket book; which he would have done had he not been prevented; others were seized in a manner equally striking.

The commander and officers of the brig

were eager to serve us, and kindly anticipated our wants. They had just snatched us from death, by rescuing us from our raft; their reiterated care rekindled in us the flame of life. Mr. Renaud, the surgeon, distinguished himself by indefatigable zeal; he passed the whole day in dressing our wounds; and during the two days that we remained on board the brig, he exerted all the resources of his art, with a degree of attention and gentleness which merit our eternal gratitude.

It was, in truth, time that our sufferings should have an end: they had already lasted thirteen days; the strongest among us might, at the most, have lived forty-eight hours more. Mr. Corréard, felt that he must die in the course of the day; yet he had a foreboding that we should be saved; he said that a series of events so extraordinary was not destined to be buried in oblivion: that providence would preserve some of us at least, to present to mankind the affecting picture of our unhappy adventures.

Through how many terrible trials have we past! Where are the men who can say that they have been more unfortunate than we have?

The manner in which we were saved is truly miraculous: the finger of heaven is conspicuous in this event.

The Argus had been dispatched, from Senegal, to assist the shipwrecked people belonging to the boats, and to look for the raft; for several days it sailed along the coast without meeting us, and gave provisions to the people from the boats who were crossing the great desert of Zaara; the captain, thinking that it would be useless to look for our raft any longer, steered his course towards the harbour from which he had been dispatched, in order to announce that his search had been fruitless; it was when he was running towards Senegal that we perceived him. In the morning he was not above forty leagues from the mouth of the river, when the wind veered to the South West; the captain, as by a kind of inspiration, said that they ought to go about, the winds blew towards the frigate; after they had run two hours on this tack, the man at the mast head, announced a vessel: when the brig was nearer to us, by the aid of glasses, they perceived that it was our raft. When we were taken up by the Argus, we asked this question: Gentlemen have you been long looking for us? We were answered yes; but that, however, the captain had not received any positive orders on the subject; and that we were indebted to chance alone, for the good fortune of having been met with. We repeat with pleasure the expression of Mr. Parnajon, addressed to one of us. " If they were " to give me the rank of captain of a fri- " gate, I should feel a less lively pleasure, " than that which I experienced when I " met your raft." Some persons said to us without reserve, " We thought you were all " dead a week ago." We say that the commander of the brig had not received positive orders to look for us. The following were his instructions: " Mr. de Parnajon, " commanding the brig Argus, will proceed " to the side of the desert with his vessel, " will employ every means to assist the " shipwrecked persons, who must have " reached the coast; and will supply them " with such provisions and ammunition as " they may want; after having assured him-

" self of the fate of these unfortunate per-
" sons, he will endeavour to continue his
" course to the Medusa, to see whether the
" currents have carried the raft towards her."
This is all that was said of our wretched machine. It is very certain, that, at the Island of St. Louis, we were given up; our friends believed we had perished: this is so true, that some, who were going to send letters to Europe, wrote that one hundred and fifty unfortunate people had been placed on a raft, and that it was impossible they should have escaped. It will not, perhaps, be out of place, to mention here a conversation which took place respecting us. In a pretty large company, some persons said: " It is
" a pity that the raft was abandoned; for
" there were many brave fellows on board;
" but their sufferings are over; they are
" happier than we, for who knows how all
" this will end." In short, as we were now found, the frigate steered again for Senegal, and the next day we saw the land, for which we had been longing for thirteen days: we cast anchor in the evening off the coast, and in the morning, the winds being favorable, we directed our course to the road of

St. Louis, where we cast anchor on the 19th of July, about three o'clock in the afternoon.

Such is the faithful history of one hundred and fifty persons, who were left upon the raft; only fifteen of whom were saved; and five of that number were so reduced, that they died of fatigue, shortly after arriving at St. Louis; those who still exist are covered with scars, and the cruel sufferings which they have endured have greatly impaired their constitution.

In terminating this recital of the unparalelled sufferings, to which we were a prey for thirteen days, we beg leave to name those who shared them with us:

Alive when we were saved.	*Notice of their subsequent fate.*
Messrs.	
Dupont, Captain of Foot;	In Senegal.
L'Heureux, Lieutenant;	In Senegal.
Lozach, Sub-Lieutenant;	Dead.
Clairet, Sub-Lieutenant;	Dead.
Griffon du Bellay, Ex-Clerk of the Navy;	Out of employment.
Coudin, *élève de marine;*	Midshipman.
Charlot, Serjeant Major; (of Toulon)	In Senegal.
Courtade, Master Gunner;	Dead.
Lavillette,	In France.
Coste, Sailor;	In France.
Thomas, Pilot;	In France.
François, Hospital Keeper;	In the Indies.
Jean Charles, black Soldier;	Dead.
Corréard, Engineer Geographer;	Without employment.
Savigny, Surgeon.	Resigned.

The governor having been apprised of our arrival, sent a large-decked vessel to convey us ashore. This vessel also brought us wine and some refreshments; the master, thinking the tide sufficiently high to enable him to pass the bar of sand, which lies at the mouth of the river, resolved to land us at once upon the island. Those who were the most feeble among us, were placed below deck, together with a few of the least skilful of the negroes, who composed the crew, and the hatches closed upon us, to prevent the sea from coming in between decks, while the dangers occasioned by the surf running over the bar, was passed. The wretched condition to which we were reduced, was such as to awaken a feeling of sympathy, even among the blacks, who shed tears of compassion for our misfortunes; during this time, the most profound silence reigned on board; the voice of the master alone was heard; as soon as we were out of danger, the negroes recommenced their songs, which did not cease till we arrived at St. Louis.

We were received in the most brilliant manner; the governor, several officers, both English and French, came to meet us, and one of the officers in this numerous train, held out to us a hand, which a fortnight before, had, as it were, plunged us in the depth of despair by loosening the tow-rope which made our raft fast to the boat. But such is the effect produced by the sight of wretches who have just been miraculously delivered, that there was not a single person, either English or French, who did not shed tears of compassion on seeing the deplorable condition to which we were reduced; all seemed truly affected by our distress, and by the intrepidity which we had shewn on the raft. Yet we could not contain our indignation, at the sight of some persons in this train.

Some of us were received by two French merchants, who bestowed on us every attention, and rendered every assistance in their power. Messrs. Valentin and Lasalle stimulated by that natural impulse which incites man to assist a fellow creature in distress, is, on that account, entitled to the highest praise. We are extremely sorry to say that they were the only colonists who gave assistance to the shipwrecked people belonging to the raft.

Before we proceed to the second part of our work, in which we shall include the history of the Camp of Daccard and of the unfortunate persons shipwrecked in the Medusa, who remained in the hospitals of St. Louis, let us cast our eyes back, and examine what were the operations of the boats after the tow-lines had been loosened, and the raft abandoned.

The long-boat was the last which we lost sight of. It descried the land and the Isles of Arguin, the same evening before sun-set: the other boats must, therefore, necessarily have seen it some time before, which proves, we think, that when we were abandoned, we were at a very small distance from the coast. Two boats succeeded in reaching Senegal without accident; they were those in which were the governor and the commander of the frigate. During the bad weather, which forced the other boats to make the land, these two had a great deal of difficulty to resist a heavy sea and an extremely high wind. Two young seamen gave proofs of courage and coolness in these critical moments, in the barge.

Mr. Barbotin, *élève* of the marine: and in the captain's barge, Mr. Rang,* also an *élève* of the marine, as deserving of praise for his knowledge, as for the courage he displayed on this occasion; both of them, as long as the bad weather lasted, remained at the helm, and guided the boats. One Thomas, steersman, and one Lange, the boatswain's mate, also shewed great courage, and all the experience of old seamen. These two boats, reached the *Echo* corvette, on the 9th, at 10 o'clock in the evening, which had been at anchor for some days, in the road of St. Louis. A council was held, and the most prompt and certain measures adopted to assist those who were left on board the boats and the raft.

---

* The conduct of this young man merits some recompense. At the end of 1816, there was a promotion of 80 midshipmen, who were to be taken from the *élèves* who had been the longest in the service; Mr. Rang was amongst the first 70, according to the years he had been in the service, and should therefore have been named by right. In fact, it is said that he was placed on the list of Candidates; but that his name was struck out because some young men, (whom they call *protégés*) applied to the ministry, and were preferred.

The Argus brig was appointed for this mission. The commander of this vessel, burning with eagerness to fly to the assistance of his unfortunate countrymen, wanted to set sail that very moment; but causes, respecting which we shall be silent, fettered his zeal; however, this distinguished officer executed the orders which he received with uncommon activity.

Let us return to the history of the four other boats; and first, that of the principal, which was the long-boat. As soon as it descried the land, it tacked and stood out in the open sea; because it was on the shallows, and it would have been imprudent to pass the night in one metre, or one metre 30 centimetres of water; it had already grounded two or three times. On the 6th, about four o'clock in the morning, finding itself too far from the coast, and the sea very hollow, it tacked, and in a few hours saw the coast for the second time. At eight o'clock, they were extremely near, and the men ardently desiring to get on shore, sixty-three of the most resolute were landed; arms were given them, and as much biscuit as could be spared; they set out in search of Senegal, following the sea-coast. This landing was effected to the North of Cape Meric, eighty or ninety leagues from the Isle of St. Louis.(17) This vessel then stood out to sea. We will leave, for the present, these sixty-three poor people who have been landed on the sands of Cape Meric; and shall return to them in the sequel.

We will now proceed to describe the motions and fate of the other vessels. At noon, after having proceeded some miles, the long-boat saw the other vessels, and endeavoured to fall in with them; but every one distrusted the other: the long-boat did its utmost to rally them; but they employed all the means they could to avoid the meeting; even the officers assisted in working them, because some persons had asserted that the crew of the long-boat had mutinied, and had even threatened to fire on the other boats.* The long-boat, on the other

---

* This report of a mutiny, among the crew of the long-boat, began to circulate as soon as it joined the line which the boats formed before the raft. The following is what was told us: when the boats had abandoned the raft, several men, in the long-boat, subaltern officers of the troops on board, exclaimed: "*let us fire on those who fly;*"

hand, which had just landed a part of its people, advanced to inform the other boats that it was able to relieve them, in case they were too much loaded. The captain's boat and the *pirogue*, were the only ones that came within hail: at five o'clock in the afternoon the sea became hollow, and the wind very high, when the pirogue, unable to hold out against it, asked the assistance of the long-boat, which tacked and took on board the fifteen persons which that frail boat contained. At two o'clock in the afternoon, of the 8th,(18) the men, tormented by a burning thirst, and a violent hunger which they could not appease, obliged the officer, by their reiterated importunities, to make the land, which was done the same evening. His intention was to proceed to Senegal: he would doubtless have succeeded; but the cries of the soldiers and sailors, who murmured loudly, induced the measure

---

already their muskets were loaded; but the officer, who commanded, had influence enough to hinder them from executing their purpose. We have also been told that one F. a quarter-master, presented his piece at the captain of the frigate. This is all we have been able to collect concerning this pretended revolt.

that was taken, and the crew landed about forty leagues from the Island of St. Louis. The great-boat, which had approached very near the coast, and had not been able to resist the violence of the weather, being besides, destitute of provisions, had also been obliged to make the land on the 8th: the first, at five in the afternoon; the second, at eleven in the morning. The officers joined their crews, ranged them in order, and proceeded towards Senegal; but they were in distress, destitute of resources of every kind: without a guide, on a coast inhabited by barbarians: hunger and thirst cruelly tormented them; the beams of a scorching sun, reflected from the immense sandy plains, aggravated their sufferings. In the day, oppressed by excessive heat, they could scarcely move a step: it was only in the cool of the morning and the evening, that they could pursue their painful march. Having, after infinite pains, crossed the downs, they met with vast plains, where they had the good fortune to find water, by digging holes in the sand: this refreshing beverage gave them fresh life and hope.

This manner of procuring water is mentioned by many travellers, and practised in various countries. All along the coasts of Senegambia, and for some distance in land, they find, by digging in the sand to the depth of five or six feet, a white and brackish water, which is exclusively used in these countries, both for the ordinary beverage and domestic purposes; the water of the Senegal, may, however, be used at St. Louis at the time of the rise or inundation.

The Moors have signs, which they have agreed upon among themselves, to inform each other at a distance when they have found water. As the sands of the desert lie in undulations, and the surface of these plains has the appearance of a sea, broken in large waves, which, by some sudden enchantment, had been fixed and suspended before they could fall back; it is on the ridges of these motionless waves, that the Moors in general travel, unless they run in a direction too different from that of their intended route, in which case they are obliged to traverse them; but besides, as these ridges themselves are not always ranged parallel to each other, but frequently cross each other, the Moors always have some of their party before, to serve as guides, and to point out, by signs with their hands, at every crossing, on which side they ought to go; and also every thing which prudence requires they should know before hand, as well as the water, or rather the moisture and verdure which are to be perceived. In general, these people who approach the sea-coast during the winds and hurricanes of the summer solstice, rarely keep on the breach properly so called, because they and their cattle are too much tormented by myriads of flies which never quit the sea-coast. In this same season the appearance of the gnats, or mosquitoes, induces them to remove from the Senegal, for their cattle being incessantly stung by these animals, become mad and sick.

Our people met with some of these Moors, and in some measure forced them to serve as guides; after continuing their march along the sea-coast, they perceived on the morning of the 11th, the Argus brig, which was cruising to assist those who had landed; as soon as the brig perceived them, it approached very near to the coast, lay-to, and sent a boat on shore with biscuit and wine.

On the 11th, in the evening, they met with more of the natives, and an Irish captain of a merchant ship, who, of his own accord, had come from St. Louis with the intention of assisting the sufferers: he spoke the language of the country, and had put on the same dress as the Moors. We are sorry that we cannot recollect the name of this foreign officer, which we should take particular pleasure in publishing; but since time has effaced it from our memory, we will at least publish his zeal and noble efforts, which are an unquestionable title to the gratitude of every man of feeling. At last, after the most cruel sufferings and privations, the unfortunate men who composed the crews of the great-boat, and of that which we called the Senegal boat, twenty-five men from the long-boat, and fifteen persons from the pirogue, arrived at Saint Louis, on the 13th of July, at seven o'clock in the evening, after having wandered above five whole days, in the midst of these frightful deserts, which on all sides presented to their eyes only the most profound solitude, and the prospect of inevitable destruction.

During their progress, they had to struggle with the most dreadful extremes of hunger and thirst; the latter was such, that the first time that several of them discovered water in the desert, such selfishness was manifested that those who had found these beneficent springs, knelt down four or five together, near the hole which they had just dug, and there, with their eyes fixed on the water, made signs to their comrades not to approach them; that they had found the springs, and that they alone had a right to drink at them; it was not till after the most urgent supplications that they granted a little water to their wretched companions, who were consumed by a raging thirst. When they met with any Moors, they obtained some assistance from them; but these barbarians carried their inhumanity so far as to refuse to shew them the springs which are scattered along the shore: sordid avarice made them act in this manner to these unhappy people; for when the latter had passed a well, the Moors drew water from it, which they sold to them at a gourd for a glass; they exacted the same price for a small handful of millet. When the brig approached the coast, to assist these unfortunate men, a great many of the natives of the country immediately crowned the heights; their number was so great, that it caused some fear in the French, who immediately formed, in order of battle, under the command of a captain of infantry. Two officers went to ask the chiefs of the Moors what were their intentions? whether they desired peace or war? They gave the officers to understand that far from wishing to act as enemies, they were willing to afford the shipwrecked people all the assistance in their power; but these barbarians shewed, on all occasions, a perfidiousness which is peculiar to the inhabitants of these climates; when the brig had sent biscuit on shore, they seized the half of it, and a few moments after, sold it at an exorbitant price, to those from whom they had stolen it. If they met with any soldiers or sailors who had had the imprudence to stray from the main body, they stripped them entirely, and then ill treated them; it was only numbers united, which, inspiring them with fear,

that did not receive any insult from them; besides, there exists between the chiefs of these tribes and the government of the Isle of St. Louis, a treaty, in which it is stipulated that a large reward shall be given to the Moors, who meet in the desert with persons that have been shipwrecked, and bring them to the European factory: these barbarians were therefore induced by their interest, and if they brought back those who went astray, it was only in hope of obtaining a reward.

The women and young children inspired the greatest pity. These feeble beings could not put their delicate feet on the burning sands, and were besides incapable of walking for any length of time. The officers themselves assisted the children, and carried them in turn: their example induced others to imitate them; but having met with some Moors, who never travel in these deserts without having their camels and their asses with them, all that were not able to walk, mounted these animals: to obtain this indulgence, it was necessary to pay two gourds for a day; so that it was impossible for Mr. Picard, who had a numerous family, to bear so great an expence; his respectable young ladies were therefore obliged to walk.

One day at noon, which was the hour for halting, the eldest of these young ladies, exhausted with fatigue, withdrew to a solitary place to take some moments rest. She fell asleep upon the beach; to guard herself from the musquitoes, she had covered her breast and face with a large shawl. While every body was sleeping, one of the Moors who served as guides, either from curiosity, or some other motive, approached her softly, attentively examined her appearance, and not content with this, lifting up the shawl, looked at her with fixed eyes, remained for a few moments like one profoundly astonished, approached her then very near, but did not venture to touch her. After having looked at her for some time, he let fall the veil, and returned to his place, where he joyfully related to his comrades what he had just seen. Several Frenchmen who had perceived the Moor, informed Mr. Picard. who resolved, on the obliging offers of the officers, to dress these ladies in a military dress, which, for the future, prevented all attempts of the inhabitants of the desert.

Before they arrived at the Senegal, the Irish officer, of whom we have already spoken, bought an ox: it was immediately killed; they collected such combustibles as they could find, and when the animal was divided into as many portions as there were persons, each fixed his portion to the end of his sabre or bayonet, and thus they prepared a repast which they found delicious.

During the whole time they remained in the desert, biscuit, wine and brandy, in very small quantities, had been their principal nourishment; sometimes they procured by money, from the Moors, milk and millet; but what most distressed them was, that in the midst of these sandy plains, it was absolutely impossible for them to shelter themselves from the rays of a burning sun, which inflames the atmosphere of these desert regions. Scorched by insupportable heat, almost destitute of the first necessaries of life, some of them partly lost their senses; a spirit of mutiny even shewed itself for some moments, and two officers, whose conduct is, however, irreproachable, were marked as the first victims: happily they did not proceed to open violence. Many of those who crossed the desert, have assured us that there were moments when they were quite beside themselves.

An officer of the army in particular, gave signs of the most violent despair; he rolled himself in the sand, begging his comrades to kill him, because he could no longer bear up against so many sufferings. They succeeded in calming him; he arrived at St. Louis with the caravan.(20)

The sixty-three who embarked near the Moles of Angel, had a longer series of fatigue to endure: they had to go between eighty and ninety leagues, in the immense desert of Zaara. After their landing, they had to cross downs that were extremely elevated, in order to reach the plain, in which they had the good fortune to meet with a vast pond of fresh water, where they quenched their thirst, and near which they lay down to rest. Having met with some Moors, they took them for guides, and after long marches, and the most cruel privations, they arrived at the Senegal, on the 23d of July, in the evening. Some of them perished for want: among this number was an unhappy gardener, and the wife of a soldier: this poor woman, exhausted with fatigue, told her husband to abandon her, for, that it was impossible for her to proceed; the soldier in despair, said to her in a rage: " well, since you cannot walk, to hinder " you from being devoured alive by wild " beasts, or carried into captivity among " the Moors, I will run you through the " body with my sabre;" he did not execute this threat, which he had probably conceived in a moment of despair; but the poor woman fell, and died under the most cruel sufferings.

Some persons having strayed from the main body, were taken by the natives of the country, and carried into the camp of the Moors; an officer remained above a month with them, and was afterwards brought to the Isle of St. Louis. The naturalist, Kummer, and Mr. Rogery, having separated from the troops, were forced to wander from one horde to another, and were at last conducted to Senegal. Their story, which we are now going to give, will complete the narrative of the adventures of our shipwrecked companions who traversed the desart.

After the stranding of the long-boat, Mr. Kummer quitted the caravan, formed by the persons wrecked, and proceeded in an easterly direction, in the hope of meeting with some Moors, who would give him food, to appease the hunger and thirst which he had endured for two days. Shortly after his departure, Mr. Rogery took the same resolution as our naturalist, and followed a route parallel to that taken by Mr. Kummer. This latter walked the whole day without meeting with any body; towards the evening he perceived, at a distance, some fires on the heights which generally lie round the ponds. This sight filled him with joy, and with hopes of meeting, at length, with some Moors who would conduct him to the Isle of St. Louis, and give him food of which he was much in need; he advanced with a firm and rapid step, went up to the Moors, who were under their tents, with much assurance, pronouncing as well as he could, a few words in Arabic, in which language he had taken some lessons while in France, and which he accompanied with profound salutations:

"Receive," said he, "in your tents, the
"son of an unfortunate Mahometan woman,
"whom I am going to join in Upper Egypt;
"a shipwreck has thrown me on your coast,
"and I come in the name of the great
"prophet, to ask you for hospitality and
"assistance." At the name of the great
prophet, Mr. Kummer bowed his face to the
earth, and made the customary salutation:
the Moors did the same, and doubted not
but that they saw, before them, a follower
of Mahomet.

They received him with joy, asked him
to enter their tents, and to give a short
account of his adventures. Milk, and flour
of millet, were given him, and this food
revived his strength. Then the Moors made
him promise to conduct them to the place
where the long-boat had stranded; they
hoped to get possessions of the numerous effects, which they supposed the persons shipwrecked to have abandoned on the shore.
Having made this promise, Mr. Kummer
went to examine the tents, and the flocks
of the chief of this tribe who conducted
him himself, and boasted of his wealth and
his dignity: he told him that he was the

Prince Fune Fahdime Muhammed, son of Liralie Zaide, King of the Moors, called Trazas, and that, when he returned from the sea coast, he would take him to the King, his father, and that he would see there, his numerous slaves, and his innumerable flocks. While they were walking about the camp, Prince Muhammed perceived that Mr. Kummer had a watch: he desired to see it; of course, he could not refuse to shew it; the prince took it, and told Mr. Kummer that he would return it him when they should arrive at Andar, which promise he punctually performed. They arrived at last at the head of the flock, and our naturalist was astonished at the extraordinary care which these people take of their beasts. The horses and camels were in a separate place, and the whole flock was on the border of a large salt pond; behind them, the slaves had formed a line of fires of great extent, to drive away the mosquitoes and other insects, which torment these animals: they were all remakably beautiful. While traversing, with the chief, the various quarters of the camp, Mr. Kummer beheld with surprise, their manner of cleaning their beasts.

Upon an order of the Prince, the men, charged with this employment, take the strongest oxen by the horns, and throw them down on the sand with astonishing ease; the slaves then take the animal, and clear its whole body from the insects, which, notwithstanding the fires that surround the flocks, get among the hair of the cattle, which they torment cruelly. After this first operation, they are washed with care, particularly the cows, which are then milked. These various operations generally employ the slaves, and even the masters, till eleven o'clock at night. Mr. Kummer was afterwards invited to repose in the Prince's tent; but before he could go to sleep, he was assailed with a multitude of questions. The history of the French Revolution has penetrated to these people; and they put questions to our naturalist which surprised him much; they afterwards asked him why our vessels no longer came to Portendick and the Isles of Arguin; after this, they allowed him to take a few moments' repose; but the poor Toubabe, (the name which the Moors give to the whites) did not dare to indulge himself in sleep; he feared the perfidy of the Moors, and their rapacious spirit; however, exhausted by three days incessant fatigue, he fell asleep for a few moments; he had but a very disturbed slumber; during which, the barbarians took away his purse, which still contained thirty pieces of 20 francs each, his cravat, pocket handkerchief, great-coat, shoes, waistcoat, and some other things which he carried in his pockets: he had nothing left but a bad pair of pantaloons and a hunting jacket; his shoes were, however, returned to him.

The next morning, at sun-rise, the Moors made their salam, (a Mahometan prayer): then about eight o'clock, the Prince, four of his subjects, Mr. Kummer, and a slave, set out for the sea-coast, in order to look for the wreck of the long-boat. They proceeded first towards the *South*, then to the *West*, then to the *North*, which made Mr. Kummer imagine that they were conducting him to Morocco. The Moors have no other method of finding their way, than to go from one eminence to another, which obliges them to take all sorts of directions; after they had proceeded five or six leagues to the East, they again turned to the *West*, then to the *South West*. After walking a considerable time longer, they arrived at the shore, where they found but few things. What pa ticular y attracted their attention, was pieces of copper: they took them away, resolving to return and fetch the fragments of the long-boat, and several barrel, which the currents had driven on the coast. After taking whatever they could carry away, they set out towards the *East*, and at the end of about two leagues, they met some other Moors, also subjects of Prince Muhammed; they stopped and lay down under their tents: the Prince lay down under the finest, and ordered refreshments to be given to the *Toubabe*, who was worn out with fatigue and want of nourishment. Here Mr. Kummer was tormented by the women and children, who came every moment to touch and feel the fineness of his skin, and to take away some fragments of his shirt, and the few things which he had left. During the evening, fresh questions were put to him respecting the cruel wars which desolated France; he was obliged to trace the account of them, on the sand in Arabic letters. It was this extreme complaisance, and his pretended quality of the son of a Christian and of a Mahometan woman, which caused him to be upon very good terms with Prince Muhammed, and in general, with all the Moors whom he met with, on his journey. Every moment of the day, the Prince begged Mr. Kummer, to make the wheels of his watch go, the motions of which, much astonished the Moors; our traveller was on his side equally surprised, to see among the hordes, children five or six years of age, who wrote Arabic perfectly well.

The next day, July 8, at day-break, the Moors went and stationed themselves on the summit of a hill. There, prostrated with their faces turned towards the East, they waited for the rising of the sun, to perform their salam, which they begin the moment he appears in the horizon. Mr. Kummer followed them, imitated them in all their ceremonies, and never failed in the sequel, to perform his devotions at the same time as they did. The ceremony being over, the prince and his suite, continued their route in the direction of the *South East*, which again frightened the poor *Toubabe;* he thought that the Moors were going to resume their course to the *North*, and that in the end they would take him to Morocco; then he endeavoured to impart his uneasiness to Prince Muhammed, who at last comprehended him; but to make it quite clear, Mr. Kummer drew upon the sand, a part of the map of Africa; mean time, he heard them continually pronounce the word *Andar*, which did not at all diminish his alarms; but by the lines which he traced, he soon understood that the Moors meant the Isle of St. Louis; of which he was convinced when he had written the name of the European factory, by the side of that of Andar. The Moors let him know that they had comprehended him; and shewed great joy that a white could understand their language.

At noon, they stopped on the side of a great pond or lake. Mr. Kummer, who was extremely fatigued, lay down on the sand, and fell asleep immediately. During his sleep, the Moors went to look for a fruit, produced by a tree which generally grows on the sides of these lakes (marigots). They are bunches of little red berries, and very refreshing: the Moors are very fond of them, and make great use of them.*

During this time, chance ordered it, that Mr. Rogery, who had also been taken by the Moors, stopped at the same place: he was brought by some of the natives, who were taking him also to their sovereign Zaide: he soon perceived Mr. Kummer lying with his face to the earth, and thought he was dead; at this sight, a mortal chillness pervaded all the limbs of the unfortunate Rogery; he deplored the loss of a friend, of a companion in misfortune: he approached him trembling; but his grief was soon changed into joy, when he perceived that his friend still breathed; he

---

* The fruit here mentioned, is probably jujubes (ziziphum), in their last stage of maturity. The author of this note, has found in the deserts of Barbary, and the shades of the Acacias, some immense *jujubes;* but, besides this fruit, the only one of a red or reddish colour which he has remarked in this country, are those of some *caparidées*, very acid; some *icaques* before they are ripe; the *tampus* or *sebestum* of Africa, and the wood of a *prasium*, which is very common in most of the dry places: the calyx of which, is swelled, succulent, and of an orange colour, good to eat, and much sought after by the natives.

took hold of him, and embraced him eagerly. These two unfortunate men were transported with mutual joy, at meeting in the midst of their distress, with a fellow countryman. Mr. Rogery had lost every thing; they had taken from him about forty pieces of 20 francs each, his watch, and all his effects: he had nothing left but his shirt, a very bad pair of pantaloons, and a hat. The wives of the Moors, and still more the children, had greatly tormented him; the latter, continually pinched him, and hindered him from taking a moment's sleep. His character was remarkably soured by this treatment, and his faculties rather impaired. These two unfortunate men, after having related their distresses to each other, fell asleep close together; some hours after, the Moors returned, and gave them some of the berries we have before mentioned. The caravan soon set forward again, and took a *South West* direction, which led to the camp of King Zaide: they reached it in the evening, but the monarch was absent; the report of our shipwreck had reached his camp, and Zaide, who desires to see every thing himself, had gone to the sea-shore to have assistance given to such of the persons shipwrecked, as he should meet with. The King did not return till twenty-four hours after, which gave time for our travellers to repose, and for Prince Muhammed to make a bargain with the two whites: to conduct them to the Isle of St. Louis; the Prince demanded for his trouble, including the expences of provisions and travelling, 800 gourdes for each, and obliged them before they set out, to sign an agreement in the Arabic language: Mr. Kummer consented to it, and said to Mr. Rogery, when we have once got to St. Louis, we will give them what we please. The latter hesitated, being much more scrupulous on that point, he would not at first accede to an agreement which he feared he should not be able to perform; but seeing that the Moors were resolved to keep him among them, he consented to accept the absolute proposal of the Prince, and the conventions were signed.

Our two travellers passed a part of their time in examining the customs of these people; we shall mention some circumstances which particularly struck them.

They observed, that the children imperiously command their fathers and mothers: but especially the latter, who never oppose their inclinations; hence, doubtless comes that despotic spirit, which is carried to the extreme; a refusal, or a delay, in the executions of their orders irritates them, and their anger is so violent that, in the first transport, the unhappy slave who may have excited their fury, runs the risk of being stabbed on the spot. Hence, too doubtless the manly boldness which characterises them, and which seems to inspire those who surround them, with respect and submission. The Moors are, in every respect, much superior to the Negroes: braver than they are, they reduce them to slavery, and employ them in the hardest labour; they are, in general, tall and well made, and their faces are very handsome, and full of expression.

However, it may also be observed that the Moors of both sexes, appear at the first sight, like a people composed of two distinct races, which have nothing in common, except, the extremely brown, or tanned colour of their skin, and the shining black of their hair. The greater part of them, it is true, are endowed with the stature, and the noble, but austere features, which call to mind some of the great Italian painters, but there are several, (indeed the smaller number) whose cranium and profile form a singular contrast with the others. Their head is remarkably elongated, the ears small: the forehead, which, in the first, is very high and finely formed, is contracted in the latter, and becomes at the top disagreeably protuberant; their eyes are sunk, and placed as it were obliquely, which gives them the savage look with which they are reproached, and their lower jaw has a tendency to be elongated. Some of them have, it is true, the high forehead of the former: but it always differs by being sunk in at the base. These latter are, perhaps, the descendants of the aborigines of this country, whose characteristic features are still discernible, notwithstanding their alliance with so many strangers? History has, indeed, transmitted to us some of the customs of the Numidians, who were by turns, the enemies, and the allies of the Romans; but it has not condescended to draw their portrait. Juvenal somewhere speaks of the withered hands of the Moors: *manus ossea Mauri*. But, besides, that this is general in hot countries, this description may be understood of ill-fed slaves.

The travellers remarked that there was no difference between the very frugal diet of the slaves, who are all blacks, and that of their masters. The fathers and mothers, as well as the marabous, (a kind of priests) pass their leisure moments in teaching the principles of their religion, as well as instructing them in reading and writing on the sand; the wives of King Zaide, the number of whom is considerable, passively obey Fatima, who is the favourite, or chief wife of the sovereign.

Our travellers estimated the number of men, women, children and slaves, at seven or eight hundred persons; their flocks appeared to them very numerous: they constitute a part of the wealth of Zaide, who possesses a great many besides, in different parts of the kingdom, the extent of which is pretty considerable; it has about sixty leagues of coast, and stretches to a great depth in the interior of the desert. The people, as we have said, call themselves *Trasas*, and profess the Mahometan religion; they hunt lions, tigers, leopards, and all other ferocious animals, which abound in this part of Africa. Their commerce is in furs or skins, and ostrich feathers: they manufacture the leather called basil, in french, basane, which they prepare very well;(21) they make this leather into pocket-books, to which they give different forms, but in general, that of a *sabretache*. They also dress goats skins, and join several together to give them more breadth; they are known under the name of *peaux de maures*, are excellent, and afford a complete defence against the rain: in form, they nearly resemble the dress of a Capuchin; they sell all these articles in the interior, as well as goldsmiths work, which they manufacture with only a hammer, and a little anvil; but their chief commerce, which is very extensive, is in salt, which they carry to Tombuctoo, and to Sego, large and very populous cities, situated in the interior of Africa. Sego is built on both sides of the river Niger, and Tombuctoo not far from its banks, the former about five hundred, and the latter about six hundred leagues East of the Island of Goree. The Marabous, who are almost all traders, frequently extend their journeys into Upper Egypt. The Moors and the Negroes, have an extraordinary respect for these priests, who manufacture leather, into little etuis, perfumed bags, and pocket-books, to which they give the name of *gris-gris*. By means of magic words spoken over the *gris-gris*, and little notes written in Arabic, which they enclose in them, he who carries such a one about him, is secure against the bite of wild beasts; they make them to protect the wearer against lions, crocodiles, serpents, &c. They sell them extremely dear, and those who possess them set a very high value on them; the king and the princes are not less superstitious than those whom they command. There are some who wear as many as twenty of these *gris-gris* fixed to the neck, the arms, and the legs.

After a day's stay, King Zaide arrived: he had no ornament which distinguished him; but he was of a lofty stature, had an open countenance, and three large teeth in the upper jaw, on the left side, which projected at least two lines over the under lip, which the Moors consider as a great beauty. He was armed with a large sabre, a poniard and a pair of pistols; his soldiers had zagayes or lances, and little sabres in the Turkish fashion. The King has always at his side, his favourite negro, who wears a necklace of red pearls, and is called Billaï. Zaide received the two whites kindly, ordered that they should be well-treated, and that Mr. Rogery should not be molested, he being continually tormented by the children. Mr. Kummer was much more lively, and did not mind his misfortunes; he wrote Arabic, and had passed himself off for the son of a Mahometan woman; all this greatly pleased the Moors, who treated him well; while Mr. Rogery, deeply affected by his misfortunes, and having just lost his last resources, did not much rely on the good faith of the Moors.

In the course of the day, the King ordered Mr. Kummer to relate to him the events of the last French revolution; he was already acquainted with those of the first. Mr. Kummer did not exactly comprehend what the king wanted of him. Zaide ordered his chief minister, to draw upon the sand, the map of Europe, the Mediteranean, and the coast of Africa, along that sea: he pointed out to him the Isle of Elba, and ordered him to relate the circumstances which had taken place in the invasion of 1815, from the moment that Buonaparte left it. Mr. Kummer took advantage of this favorable moment, to ask for his watch; and the King ordered his son to return it to the *Toubabe*, who then commenced his narrative; and as in the course of it he called the Ex-Emperor, sometimes Buonaparte, and sometimes Napoleon, a Marabou, at the name of Buonaparte, interrupted him, and asked if he was the general whose armies he had seen in Upper Egypt, when he was going on his pilgrimage to Mecca, to which Mr. Kummer answering in the affirmative, the king and his suite were quite delighted; they could not conceive how a mere general of army had been able to raise himself to the rank of Emperor: it seems that these people had, till then, believed that Napoleon and Buonaparte were two different persons. Mr. Kummer was also asked if his father belonged to the army of Egypt:

he said no, but that he was a peaceable merchant, who had never borne arms. Mr. Kummer continued his narrative, and astonished more and more, the King of the Trasas, and all his court. The next day, Zaide desired to see the two whites again, from whom he always learnt something new. He sent away the Moors, his subjects, who had brought Mr. Rogery, and ordered his son, Prince Muhammed, accompanied by one of his ministers, two other Moors of his suite, and a slave, to conduct the two whites to Andar. They had camels to carry them, as well as their provisions. Zaide, before he dismissed them, made them take some refreshments, gave them provisions, for a part of the journey, and advised Mr. Kummer to entrust his watch to his son; because, by that means, he would be secure from its being taken from him by the Moors; and that it would be returned to him at Saint Louis. Mr. Kummer immediately obeyed. The prince faithfully executed his father's orders.

Before the departure of the two Frenchmen, the King wished to shew them his respect for the laws which govern his dominions; knowing that this quality is that which nations always desire to find in those who govern them; he therefore thought, with reason, that he could not give a higher idea of his virtues, and show his character in a more honorable light, than by convincing them that he was the protector and most faithful observer of the laws: to prove it, he related the following anecdote:

" Two princes, my subjects, had had
" an affair, for a long time, in litigation:
" to terminate it, they resolved to ask
" me to be arbitrator between them; but
" the proposals which I made, though I
" thought them reasonable, were not ap-
" proved by them; so that after my propo-
" sals, a violent quarrel arose between the
" two parties: a challenge ensued, and
" the two princes left my tent to decide
" their cause by arms. In fact, they fought
" in my presence; one of them, the weakest,
" who was my friend, was thrown down by
" his adversary, who stabbed him imme-
" diately. I had the grief to see my friend
" die, and notwithstanding all my power,
" it was impossible for me, as our laws
" allow duelling, and on account of the

" respect which I have for them, to avenge
" the death of the prince whom I esteemed.
" You may judge, by this, how scrupulously
" I observe the laws by which I govern
" my dominions, and which regulate the
" rights of the princes, as well as those of
" the citizens, and of the slaves."

The third and fourth day, after they had quitted the camp of King Zaide, our travellers were reposing as usual, till the greatest heat of the day should be passed. During the repast, the minister, who had the contracts between the Prince and the two Frenchmen, took from his great *gris-gris*, or pocket book, that of Mr. Rogery, who snatched it from him, and tore it into a thousand pieces; immediately one of the Moors rushed upon him, seized him by the throat, with one hand threw him on the ground, and was going to stab him with a dagger which he held in the other; happily, the Prince, out of regard for Mr. Kummer, whom he particularly esteemed, pardoned him who had dared, so seriously, to insult one of his ministers. But, during the four or five days that the journey continued, they incessantly tormented him; and did not give him a fourth part of what was necessary for his support, so that the unfortunate man was frequently obliged to gnaw the bones which the Moors had thrown away; they also forced him to make the whole journey on foot; it was pretty long; for these gentlemen, on their arrival at St. Louis, estimated it at a hundred and forty leagues at the least, because the Moors made them go so much out of their way.

The respectable Mr. Rogery, a man of rare probity, was disturbed by the recollection of the agreement which he had made with Muhammed, in a moment of difficulty, knowing very well that he could never fulfil it; he thought his honor implicated, and strictly bound by this contract, though he had destroyed it. This recollection, and his inability to pay, affected his nerves; to this was added fear, lest the contract should be known to his countrymen; and this was what induced him to that act of desperation which had nearly cost him his life, and deprived humanity of one of the most zealous partisans of liberty, and of the abolition of the slave trade.

On the 19th, in the morning, they arrived at a village situated on the bank of one of the arms of Senegal, which is called *Marigot of the Maringouins*, and which appears to have been the ancient mouth of the river, when it flowed directly to the sea, before it turned aside and flowed to the South. This position may one day become important, if Senegambia should ever be colonised.

The gentlemen remarked, that the banks of this arm of the river, are very well cultivated; the fields are covered with plantations of cotton-trees, with maize* and millet;

---

* Is it really maize (zea) which has been observed about this *Marigot*, in large plantations? This name is so often given to varieties of the Sorgho, or dourha of the negroes, that there is probably a mistake here. In a publication, printed since this expedition, it has been stated, that maize was cultivated in the open fields, by the negroes of Cape Verd, whereas they cultivate no species of grain, except two kinds of *houlques*, to which they add, here and there, but in smaller fields, a kind of haricot, or French bean, *dolique unguiculé*, which they gather in October, and a part of which they sell at Goree and St. Louis, either in pods or seed. The dishes which they prepare with this *dolique*, are seasoned with leaves of the Baobab, (Adansonia) reduced to powder, and of cassia, with obtuse leaves, and still fresh. As for the cous-cous, the usual food of the negroes, it is made of the

one meets, at intervals, with tufts of wood, which render it agreeable and healthy. Mr. Kummer thinks that this country could be adapted to the cultivation of colonial productions. Here begins Nigritia, and one may say, the country of good people; for, from this moment, the travellers were never again in want of food, and the negroes gave them whatever they wanted.

In the first village, which is called Vu, they met with a good negress, who offered them milk and cous-cous, (flour of millet).

---

meal of sorgho, boiled up with milk. To obtain this meal, they pound the millet in a mortar, with a hard and heavy pestle of mahogony, *(mahogon)* which grows on the banks of Senegal. The *mahogon* or *mahogoni* which, according to naturalists, has a great affinity to the family of the *miliacées*, and which approaches to the genus of the *cedrelles*, is found in India, as well as in the Gulph of Mexico, where it is beginning to grow scarce. At St. Domingo, it is considered as a species of *acajou*,** and they give it that name. The yellow *mahogoni*, of India, furnishes the satin wood. There is also the *mahogoni febrifuge*, the bark of which supplies the place of the Peruvian bark. Lamarque has observed that the *mahogon* of Senegal has only eight stamina; the other kinds have ten.

** Acajou is, we believe, generally used for mahogany.—T.

She was affected, and shed tears when she saw the two unhappy whites almost naked, and particularly when she learned that they were Frenchmen. She began by praising our nation; it is the custom of these people; and then, she gave them a short account of the misfortunes she had experienced. This good negress had been made a slave by the Moors, who had torn her from the arms of her mother; she consequently detested them, and called them the banditti of the desert; she said to the two whites, in very good French: " are they not very villainous " people? "Yes," answered our unhappy countrymen. "Well," continued she, "these " robbers carried me off, notwithstanding " the efforts of my unhappy father, who de- " fended me with courage; they then car- " ried desolation into our village, which a " moment before enjoyed tranquillity and " happiness; on this sad day we saw whole " families carried off, and we were all " conducted to that horrible market at St. " Louis, where the whites carry on the exe- " crable trade of dealers in men; chance " favored me, and saved me from being sent " to find death in America, amidst the tem-

" pests which cover the ocean that separates
" it from Africa. I had the good fortune
" to fall into the hands of the respectable
" General Blanchot,* whose name and me-

---

* The probity and justice of General Blanchot were so fully appreciated by the inhabitants of St. Louis, that when his death deprived the colony of its firmest support, all the merchants and officers of the government united to raise a monument to him, in which the remains of this brave general still repose. It was a short time after his death that the English took possession of St Louis, and all the officers of that nation joined in defraying the expences of the erection of the monument, on which there is an epitaph beginning with these words: " *Here repose the remains of the brave and upright General Blanchot,*" &c. We think it not foreign to the purpose, to publish a trait which will prove how far General Blanchot carried his ideas of justice; every man, of sensibility, reads with pleasure, the account of a good action, particularly when it belongs to an hero of his own nation.

Some time before Senegal was given up to the English, St. Louis was strictly blockaded, so that all communication with France was absolutely impossible; in a short time the colony was short of all kinds of provisions. The prudent general called an extraordinary council, to which he invited all the chief inhabitants of the town, and the officers of government. It was resolved not to wait till the colony was destitute of provisions; and that, in order to hold out to the last extremity, all the inhabitants, without distinction of colour, or of rank, should have only a quarter of a ration of bread, and two ounces of rice

"mory will be ever dear to the inhabitants
"of St. Louis. This worthy governor kept
"me some years in his service; but seeing
"that I always thought of my country and

---

or millet per day; to execute this decree, all the provisions were removed into the government magazines, and the general gave orders that it should be punctually followed. Some days after these measures were taken, the governor, according to his custom, invited the authorities to dine with him; it was understood that every one should bring his portion of bread and of rice; nevertheless, a whole loaf was served up on the governor's table. As soon as he perceived it, he asked his servants who could have given orders to the store-keeper to suspend, in respect to himself, the decree of the general council? All the company then interfered, and said that the council had never had any idea of putting him upon an allowance, and that he ought to permit this exception. The General, turning to one of his aides-de-camp, said: "go and tell the store-keeper,
" that I put him provisionally under arrest, for having
" exceeded my orders; and you, gentlemen, know that I
" am incapable of infringing on the means of subsistance
" of the unhappy slaves, who would certainly want food,
" while I had a superfluous supply on my table: learn that
" a French general knows how to bear privations, as well
" as the brave soldiers under his command." During the short time of the scarcity, which lasted four months, the General would never permit a larger ration to be given to him, than that which came to the meanest slave; his example prevented every body from murmuring, and the colony was saved. While they were suffering the severest

" my relations, and that, in short, I could
" not habituate myself to your customs, he
" gave me my liberty, and from that mo-
" ment I have vowed eternal friendship to
" every thing that bears the French name."
Our two whites were much affected by this
interesting meeting; from that moment
they fancied themselves among their own
countrymen.

After some hours repose they continued their journey, and in fact, they had every reason to praise the negroes, who did not let them want for anything. In proportion, as they approached the town, the Moors became much more civil, and when they were going to pass the river, to enter St. Louis, Prince Muhammed returned

---

privations the harvest was approaching, and, at length, delivered St. Louis from the scarcity. At the same time, vessels arrived from France, and brought abundant supplies. But soon after, the English returned to besiege St. Louis, and made themselves master of it. Though this note has carried us rather away from our subject, we would not pass over in silence, so honorable a trait; it is a homage paid to the memory of the brave General Blanchot. We may add, that after having been governor, during a long series of years, he died without fortune. How few men do we find who resemble Blanchot?

Mr. Kummer his watch. The French governor received the Prince and his suite, very well; he caused them to be paid about sixty francs in two sous-pieces; this sum seemed enormous to them; for they were extremely satisfied with it: this gives ground to suppose that they were not acquainted with the value of the gourde, when they demanded eight hundred for the ransom of each of the two travellers. It was on the 22nd of July, that they arrived, after having wandered sixteen days in the burning desert of Zaara, and having endured all the horrors of hunger and thirst, particularly the unfortunate Mr. Rogery, who had to bear all the caprices of the Moors.

All the shipwrecked persons who had escaped these disasters being assembled at St. Louis, we thought we should immediately take possession of our establishments. But the English governor, Mr. Beurthonne, having learned our shipwreck, either of his own authority, or having received orders to that effect, from his government, refused to give up the colony. This difficulty obliged the commander of the French expedition to take measures, to wait for fresh orders from France. He was enjoined to send away immediately all the shipwrecked persons who arrived in the town of St. Louis.

Every thing induces us to believe that the delay in the restitution of these settlements depended on the English governor, who threw obstacles in the way, whenever circumstances permitted him. He alledged at first, that he had not received orders to give up the colony, and that besides he was in want of vessels to remove his troops, and all the effects belonging to his nation. This last allegation of wanting vessels is, of itself, sufficient to shew, that he was not much inclined to retire from the Isle of St. Louis; for the French governor, in order to remove all difficulties, proposed the *Loire* to serve as a transport, and this offer was refused. We think we have guessed the cause of this delay in the restitution of the colony, for two reasons, which seem to us the better founded, as they take their origin in the British policy, which is constantly to follow no other rule than its political or commercial interest. We give them, however, only as suppositions; but these suppositions seem so well confirmed by the events to which they relate, that we do not hesitate to lay them before our readers.

We think then that Mr. Beurthonne had received orders to give up the Islands of St. Louis and Goree, to the French squadron, which should come to take possession of them; but we think also, that he was desired to evacuate them as late as possible, in case the English merchants or government could derive any advantage from a delay.

In fact, if Mr. Beurthonne had not received any instructions to deliver up the colony, it was certainly, useless to alledge that he was in want of vessels. To the desires of the French governor, he had only to make the plain and unanswerable objection, that his government had not given him any orders. It is therefore, by the kind of vacillation which appears in his answers, that himself, leads us to the opinion which we have formed. But it will be said, what advantage could the English government derive from this delay? The following, is what we conjecture on this subject.

The gum trade was on the point of commencing; it was very just that the English merchants, who were in Senegal, should carry off this crop, which would have belonged to the French merchants if the colony, had been restored.

A second motive, not less powerful, is, that we were just at the entrance of the bad season, and that the English settlements, on the river Gambia, (to which, a part of the English, garrison were to go) are extremely unhealthy: diseases that are almost always mortal, prevail during the winter-season, and generally carry off two thirds of the Europeans, who are newly arrived. Every year the mortality is the same; because, every year it is necessary to send fresh garrisons: those who have the good fortune to resist these terrible epidemics, come, to recover, to the Isle of Goree, where the air is salubrious. Such are the reasons which, as we think, caused the delay in the restitution of our settlements on the coast of Africa.

Without losing ourselves farther in conjectures, we will conclude with one remark: namely, them on this occasion the English governor was influenced more by the usual policy of his government than by local and particular considerations. Let us remember what passed on the restitution of our colonies at the peace of 1802 and that of 1814; and it will be seen that the British Government, without giving itself much trouble to assign reasons, has adopted and faithfully followed the principle, of not willingly giving up what it possessed.*

The shipwreck of the Medusa favoured the designs of the governor; for, what sensation could be produced by the arrival of an expedition, of which the principal vessel no longer existed, and the three others appeared one after the other? If the English had had the intention to restore the colony on our arrival, the disorder in which we appeared, would alone have sufficed, to make them conceive the idea of delaying as much as possible to withdraw from the Island of St. Louis. But what we cannot conceive is, that the governor, after giving the French a good

---

* Every body knows the popular proverb, which very well expresses our idea: "*That which is worth taking, is worth keeping.*

reception for some days, should have required their troops to be sent away from the colony: and what were these troops? wretches almost naked, worn out by the long fatigues and privations which they had had to bear in the deserts; they were almost all without arms. Did he fear the spirit of the colonists, and even that of the negroes, which was not in his favor, and who saw with the greatest pleasure the arrival of the French? This is not at all probable.

All the shipwrecked persons being assembled at St. Louis, as we have already said, the governor, two days before his departure for Cape Verd, thought of sending a vessel on board the Medusa, to look for a sum of 100,000 francs,* which was intended

---

* It will hardly be believed to how many popular reports, these 100,000 francs have given rise. There are people who do not believe that they were ever embarked on board the frigate. How do they explain this supposition? It is by asking how the conduct of persons, who had sold the interest of their country, and their honor, to foreign interests, would have been different from that of certain persons? For our part, we do not doubt but that this report is a fable. The folly, the pride, the obstinacy, which conducted us on the bank of Arguin, have no need of having another crime added to them. Besides, if there are, sometimes, persons who sell their honor, there are

to form the treasure of the colony, as well as provisions, which were in abundance on board, and of which there was some scarcity in the colony. Very little was said about the men, who had remained on board, and to whom their companions had solemnly promised to send for them as soon as they should arrive at St. Louis; but these unfortunate men were already hardly thought of any more. Mr. Corréard says that the first day that he took a walk in the town, he went to pay a visit to the family of the governor. During the conversation, the vessel was mentioned, that was going to be sent to the Medusa, as also the possibility of recovering the 100,000 francs, provisions, and effects. Seeing that they said nothing of the seventeen men who had remained on board the frigate, he said, "but a more "precious object, of which nothing is said, is "the seventeen poor men who were left?" " Pooh, answered somebody, "seventeen! " there are not three left." " And if there

---

none who, at the same time, sell their lives; and those whom people would accuse of something more than extreme incapacity, have sufficiently proved in dangers which threatened themselves, that they well knew how to provide for their own safety.

" remained but three, but one," replied he, " yet, his life is more valuable than all that " can be recovered from the frigate ;" and left the company in anger.

When in the first part of this work, we represented Mrs. and Miss Schmalz, as alone unmoved when the frigate ran aground; and seeming to rise above the general consternation, our readers may have given them credit for uncommon greatness of soul, and more than manly courage. Why are we obliged to destroy this honorable illusion which we may have caused? Why, when these ladies, have carried indifference so far as to dispense themselves from the most common duties of humanity, by refraining from paying the smallest visit to the poor wretches, placed in the hospital at St. Louis, have they themselves discovered to, us that their composure on board the frigate was nothing but profound insensibility?

We could, however, if not excuse, at least explain this last mark of their hard-heartedness: what sight, in fact, awaited them in this melancholy abode, on the new theatre, where the sad victims of a first act of inhumanity, had to struggle with the fresh miseries prepared for them by the indifference, the inattention of their fellow-creatures? The sight of men, who all bore in their hearts, the remembrance of the faults, of a husband, of a father, could not be an object which they would be desirous of seeking, or meeting with; and in this point of view, the care, which they took to avoid the hospital, seems to us almost pardonable. But what is not, what cannot be excused, what we have not learned without the greatest surprise is, that Miss Schmalz, judging of us doubtless, after a manner of thinking which was not ours, and not supposing it possible that the faults of her father, and the inhuman conduct of herself and her mother, should not be one day known in France, should have hastened to anticipate this publication, by writing to her friends at Paris, a letter justifying her relations with the shipwrecked persons belonging to the raft, and trying to devote these unfortunate men to public hatred and contempt. In this singular letter, which has been circulated in Paris, she confessed that the sight of the shipwrecked persons inspired her with a degree of horror, which she could not suppress. "It was really impossible for me," said she, "to endure the presence of these men, without feeling a sentiment of indignation."

What then was our crime in the eyes of Miss Schmalz? Doubtless that of knowing too well the persons really guilty of our misfortunes. Yes, on this account, whenever Miss Schmalz saw us, which was extremely seldom, our presence must have been a thunder-bolt to her. She could say to herself, "these men have in their hands the fate of my father. If they speak, if if they utter complaints which they suppress here, if they are listened to, (and how should they not be listened to in a country, where a charter, the noble present of our august Monarch, causes justice and the law to reign,) instead of being the daughter of a governor, I am but a wretched orphan; instead of these honors, with which it gives me so much pleasure to be surrounded, I fall into the degradation, and the oblivion which generally await the unhappy family of a great criminal."

It is certain that, if we had listened to

our griefs, if we had called to legal account, the authors of our misfortunes, it is difficult to believe that they would have escaped the inflexible rigour of justice. But we have been generous, and it is we who are oppressed! Thus, as the historians of the human heart, have but too often observed, "*It is more easy to pardon the injury we have received, than that we have inflicted.*"

The little vessel chosen to go to the frigate, was a schooner, commanded by a lieutenant of the navy; the crew was composed of some black-drivers, and some passengers. It sailed from St. Louis, on the 26th, of July, and had on board, provisions for eight days: so that having met with contrary winds, it was obliged to return to port, after having, in vain, endeavoured for seven or eight days, to get to the Medusa.

This schooner sailed again after having taken in provisions for about twenty-five days; but, as the sails were in a very bad condition, and the owner would not change them, till they were wholly unfit for service, she was obliged to sail again, with a few repairs only. Having experienced at sea, a pretty heavy gale, the sails were almost entirely destroyed, and she was obliged to return to port after having been a fortnight at sea, without having been able to accomplish her purpose. She was then furnished with new sails, which cost about ten days labour. As soon as she was ready, they sailed for the third time, and reached the Medusa, fifty-two days, after she had been abandoned.

A very obvious reflection here presents itself to the most inattentive mind: it is certain, that the reader must presume, that this was the only schooner in the colony; it is our duty to undeceive him: many other merchants offered their vessels; but their offers were declined. The governor liked better to treat with a single house, than to have accounts to regulate with a part of the merchants of the colony; who, however, were ready to place at his disposal, every thing in their power. Mr. Durecur was the merchant favored. This house carries on the whole trade of Senegal; its firm has taken place of the African company. He made the governor large advances, both of provisions and money, which amounted to 50,000 francs; he had continually, at his house, Mr. Schmalz, his family and a numerous suite. The general opinion was that, Mr. Durecur had got by his acts of generosity, a decent profit of a hundred per cent; he was, besides, recompenced, on the application of the governor, by that decoration, which it seems, ought to be conferred for some brilliant action,* and not for a very profitable commercial transaction; but let us return to our schooner. What was the astonishment of those on board her, at still finding in the Medusa, three unfortunate men on the point of expiring! Most certainly, they were very far from expecting this meeting; but as we have said, 17 were abandoned. What became of the 14 others? We will try to relate the story of their unhappy fate.

As soon as the boats and the raft had left the frigate, these 17 men endeavoured to subsist till assistance should be sent them. They searched wherever the water had not penetrated, and succeeded in collecting sufficient biscuit, wine, brandy, and bacon, to enable them to subsist for some time. As long as their pro-

---

* Probably the cross of the legion of honor.—T.

vision lasted, tranquillity prevailed among them: but forty-two days passed without their receiving the assistance which had been promised them; when twelve of the most resolute, seeing that they were on the point of being destitute of everything, determined to get to the land. To attain their object, they formed a raft with the pieces of timber which remained on board of the frigate, the whole bound together like the first, with strong ropes: they embarked upon it, and directed their course towards the land; but how could they steer on a machine, that was doubtless destitute of oars and the necessary sails. It is certain that these poor men, who had taken with them but a very small stock of provisions, could not hold out long, and that, overcome by despair and want, they have been the victims of their rashness. That such was the result of their fatal attempt, was proved by the remains of their raft, which were found on the coast of the desert of Zaara, by some Moors, subjects of King Zaide, who came to Andar to give the information. These unhappy men were doubtless the prey of the sea-monsters which are found in great numbers on the coasts of Africa.

Unhappy victims we deplore the rigour of your lot: like us, you have been exposed to the most dreadful torments: like us abandoned upon a raft, you have had to struggle with those pressing wants which man cannot subdue, hunger and thirst carried to the extreme! Our imagination carries us to your fatal machine; we see your despair, your rage; we appreciate the whole extent of your sufferings, and your misfortunes draw forth our tears. It is then true that misfortune strikes more forcibly him who has had already to struggle with adversity! The happy man scarcely believes in misfortune, and often accuses him whose distresses he has caused.

A sailor who had refused to embark upon the raft, attempted also to reach the shore some days after the first; he put himself on a chicken coop, but he sunk within half a cable's length of the frigate.

Four men resolved not to leave the Medusa, alledging that they preferred dying on board, to braving new dangers which it seemed impossible for them to surmount. One of the four had just died when the schooner arrived, his body had been thrown into the sea: the three others were very weak; two days later they would have been no more. These unhappy men occupied each a separate place, and never left it but to fetch provisions, which in the last days consisted only of a little brandy, tallow, and salt pork. When they met, they ran upon each other brandishing their knives. As long as the wine had lasted with the other provisions, they had kept up their strength perfectly well; but as soon as they had only brandy to drink they grew weaker every day.*

---

* These desertions are unhappily too frequent in naval history. The *St. John the Baptist* stranded in 1760 on the isle of Sables, where 87 poor people were abandoned, in spite of the promises to come and fetch them, made by 320 of the shipwrecked persons, who almost all saved themselves upon the island of Madagascar. Eighty negroes and negresses perished for want of assistance, some of hunger, some in attempting to save themselves upon rafts. Seven negresses and a child who lived there for fifteen years, were exposed to the most terrible distresses, and were saved in 1776 by Mr. de Trommelin, commanding the Dauphine corvette.

The Favorite, commanded by Captain Moreau, fell in

Every care was bestowed on these three men that their situation demanded, and all three are now in perfect health.

After having given the necessary succours to the three men of whom we have just spoken, they proceeded to get out of the frigate, every thing that could be removed; they cut a large hole in her, (*on la saborda,*) and were thus able to save wine, flour, and many other things. Mr. Corréard had the simplicity to think that the shipwrecked people were going to recover a part, at least, of their effects, since a vessel,

---

with the island of Adu in 1767; he sent a boat on shore with a crew of eight men, commanded by Mr. Rivière, a navy officer, but Moreau abandoned them, because the currents drove him towards the island; and he returned to the isle of France, where he took no step to induce the government to send them assistance. The brave Rivière and all his sailors succeeded in saving themselves on the coast of Malabar, by means of a raft and his boat; he landed at Cranganor, near Calicut.

One may conceive that at the first moment the presence of danger may derange the senses, and that then people may deesrt their companions on board a vessel; but not to go to their assistance, when the danger is surmounted, not to hasten to fly to their relief, this is inconceivable.

belonging to the king, had reached the frigate. But far from it! Those who were on board declared themselves corsairs, and pillaged, as we may say, all the effects which they could get at. One of them Mr.*****, carried off several portmanteaus, and four hammocks, full of all kind of articles, the whole for his own use.

The schooner having quite completed its cargo, and all attempts to recover the 100,000 francs, of which we have spoken, being fruitless, returned to Senegal. We saw this little vessel arrive, and our hearts beat with joy; we thought we should see again our unfortunate companions, who had been abandoned on board the frigate, and recover some clothes, of which we were in much need. The schooner passed the bar, and in an hour or two had traversed the space which separated it from us. In an instant we ran to the port, and enquired if any of our unfortunate countrymen had been saved. We were answered, three are still living, and fourteen have died since our departure: this answer confounded us. We then asked if it had been possible to save any of our effects; and were answered *yes,*

P

but that they were a *good prize;* we could not understand this answer, but it was repeated to us, and we learnt for the first time that we were at war with Frenchmen, because we had been excessively unfortunate.

The next day the town was transformed into a public fair, which lasted at least a week. There were sold effects belonging to the State, and those of the unhappy crew who had perished; here, the clothes of those who were still living, a little further was the furniture of the captain's cabin: in another place were the signal flags, which the negroes were buying to make themselves aprons and cloaks; at one place they sold the tackling and sails of the frigate, at another bed-linen, frames, hammocks, quilts, books, instruments, &c. &c.

But there is one thing that is sacred, respected by every man who serves with honor, the rallying sign under which he ought to find victory or death, the flag; what it will be asked became of it?...It was saved...Did it fall into the hands of a Frenchman?...No! he who debases a respectable sign, which represents a nation, cannot belong to that nation. Well! this sign was employed in domestic uses.* Vases which belonged to the captain of the frigate himself, were also saved, and were transferred from his side-board to the table of the Governor, where Mr. de Chaumareys recognized them, and it is from him we have received these details. It is true that the ladies of the Governor had received them, as a present, from those who went on board the schooner.

Nothing was now seen in the town but negroes dressed, some in jackets and pantaloons, some in large grey great coats; others had shirts, waistcoats, *police-bonnets*, &c. every thing, in short, presented the image of disorder and confusion. Such was a part of the mission of the schooner: the provisions, which it brought, were of the greatest choice to the French Governor, who began to be in want of them.

Some days after, the Merchants of St. Louis, were authorized to go on board the

---

* Persons whom we could name, divided the great flag, and cut it up into table-cloths, napkins, &c. we mention with the distinction which they deserve, Sophia, a negress, belonging to the governor, and Margaret, a white servant.

Medusa with their vessels, on the following conditions: they were to equip the vessels at their own expence, and all the effects which they could save out of the frigate were to be divided into two equal parts, one for the government, the other for the owners of the vessels. Four schooners sailed from St. Louis, and in a few days reached their destination: they brought back to the colony a great quantity of barrels of flour, salt, meat, wine, brandy, cordage, sails, &c. &c. This expedition was terminated in less than twenty days. As the schooners arrived in the Senegal, the proper way would have been to unload them, and deposit the things saved, in a magazine, till the arrival of the French Governor, who was absent; it appears to us, that, in making the division, his presence, or that of some other competent authority was necessary. But whether the ship-owners, would not wait for the return of the Governor, or whether they were in haste to possess their share of the cargo, they went to Mr. Potin Agent, or Partner of the house of Durecur, and begged him to divide the articles saved from the frigate. We are ignorant whether Mr. Potin was authorized to make this division; but whether he was authorised or not, we think he could not make it, without the co-operation of one or more officers of the administration, since he was himself one of the ship-owners. It would have been the more easy to have this division superintended by an officer of the government, as there were then three or four at St. Louis; among whom were the secretary and the paymaster. Yet neither of them was called in to be present at these operations, though they lasted some days. However, those to whom the vessels belonged, shewed themselves much more generous to the shipwrecked people, than those who went on board the frigate, with the first schooner: the few books and effects which they had been able to save were restored to such of the crew as claimed them.

A short time after these depredations were ended, some French officers and soldiers, belonging as well to the land as the sea-service, and who were still at St. Louis, received orders from the English Governor to go immediately to the camp of Daccard: it was about the first of October. At this time Mr. Corréard remained the only Frenchman in the hospital at St. Louis, till he should be entirely recovered. We are entirely ignorant of the reasons which induced this Governor to employ such severe measures towards about twenty unhappy persons, among whom three officers had been part of the crew of the fatal raft. He however, allowed the civil officers to remain in the city.

Let us take a rapid survey of the new misfortunes which overtook some of the unfortunate persons who escaped from the raft and the desert, and remained plunged in a horrid hospital without assistance, and without consolation, before we proceed to the history of the camp at Daccard, which will terminate this account. Our readers will remember that it was on the 23d of July, that the men, who escaped from the raft, were united to the sixty-three landed by the long boat, near the Moles of Angel.

Mr. Coudin, commander of the raft, and Mr. Savigny, were received at Senegal by Mr. Lasalle, a French Merchant, who, on all occasions, bestowed on them the most generous care, which spared them the new sufferings, to which their companions in misfortune were exposed, and gives Mr. Lasalle a title to their lasting gratitude.

As for Mr. Corréard, as soon as he was at the isle of St. Louis, he and some others of our companions covered with wounds, and almost without life, were laid upon truck-beds, which, instead of mattresses, had only blankets doubled in four, with sheets disgustingly dirty; the four officers of the troops were also placed in one of the rooms of the hospital, and the soldiers and sailors in another room, near the first, and lying in the same manner as the officers. The evening of their arrival, the Governor, accompanied by the captain of the frigate, and by a numerous suite, came to pay them a visit: the air of compassion, with which he addressed them, much affected them; in this first moment, they were promised a guinea, linen to clothe them, wine to restore their strength, and ammunition to amuse them when they should be able to go out. Vain promises! It is to the compassion of strangers, alone, that they were indebted for their existence for five months. The Governor announced his departure for the camp at Duccard, saying to these poor men who were left behind, that he had given orders that they should want for nothing during his absence. All the French, able to embark, departed with the Governor.

Left to themselves in the horrid abode which they inhabited, surrounded with men in whom their cruel situation inspired no pity, our countrymen again abandoned, gave vent to their distress in useless complaints. In vain they represented to the English physician that the ordinary ration of a common soldier, which had been hitherto given them, was wholly unfit for them, first, because their health required, if it was indeed wished to recover them, better nourishment than is given to a soldier in good health in his barracks: that, besides, officers enjoyed in all countries some preference, and that, in consequence, he was requested to have regard to the just desires of the sick.

The doctor was inexorable: he answered that he had received no orders and that he should make no change. They then addressed their complaints to the English Governor, who was equally insensible. It is, however, probable that the French Governor, before his departure, had requested this officer to afford all the assistance which the situation of those whom he left required, under the protection of his generosity. If this request was made it must be allowed that this Mr. Beurthonne has a heart but little accessible to sentiments of humanity.

What a contrast between the conduct of this Lieutenant-Colonel, and that of the other officers of his nation, belonging to the expedition for exploring the interior of Africa, with whom the officers of the garrison joined. It is to their generous efforts that the officers saved from the raft, owed assistance and perhaps life. It is not, in fact, rare to see the same circumstances give rise to the same observation. On occasions of this kind, a great number of private Englishmen excite astonishment by the excess of their generosity to their enemies, while on the other hand the agents of the government, and individuals, who doubtless believe that they enter into its views, seem to glory in a conduct diametrically opposite.

These gentlemen, some days after the arrival of our unfortunate comrades, having been informed of their melancholy situation, came to the hospital and took away with them the four officers who were already able to go out; they invited them to share their repast with them, till the colony should be given up.* Forty days had passed, since the compassionate English had come to the relief of these four companions in misfortune, without the distressed Corréard's having personally felt the effects of their kindness. His health was greatly impaired, in consequence of the unheard-of sufferings which he had experienced on the raft; his wounds gave him great pain, and he was obliged to remain in the infirmary: add to this the absolute want of clothes, having nothing to cover him except the sheet of his bed, in which he wrapped himself up. Since the departure of the governor, he had heard nothing of the French, which made him very uneasy, and doubled his desire to join his countrymen, hoping to find from

---

* They dined almost every day with the English officers; but in the evening they were obliged to return to the fatal hospital, where an infinite number of victims languished: if, by chance, one of the convalescents failed to come, their generous and benevolent hosts sent to the hospital, anxiously enquiring the cause of his absence.

them, consolation and relief; for he had friends among the officers and passengers who were at the Camp of Deccard. He was in this temper of mind, and in the melancholy situation which we have just described, reduced to the ration of a common soldier, during the forty days which had just elapsed, when he caused the captain of an American merchant vessel to be asked whether he would do him the pleasure to take him to Cape Verd, to which place he was to go; the answer was affirmative, and the departure fixed for two days after. In this interval, Mr. Kummer, the naturalist, happened to express, in the presence of Major Peddy, commander in chief of the English expedition for the interior of Africa, the fears which he felt at the departure of his friend, alledging that he was very uneasy respecting the effects of the bad air of the camp of Deccard, on a constitution so shaken as that of Mr. Corréard. Searcely had the sensible Mr. Kummer ceased speaking, when Major Peddy hastily went away, returned to his apartment, and immediately got ready linen, clothes and money, and while he was thus employed, this genuine philanthropist shed tears at the fate of the unhappy man, whom he did not know, cursing those who had cruelly abandoned him. His indignation was excited, because he had been assured that ever since the departure of the French governor, Mr. Corréard had heard nothing farther, either of him, or of his countrymen. Respectable Major! worthy friend of humanity! in departing for the interior of Africa, you have carried with you the regret and the gratitude of a heart, on which your noble beneficence is indelibly engraven.

While this unexpected relief was preparing Mr. Corréard, seated at the foot of his truck bed, was overwhelmed by the thoughts of his wretchedness, and plunged in the most heart-rending reflections. All that he saw affected him still more deeply, than the dreadful scenes which had passed upon the raft. " In the very heat of battle, said he, " the pain of my wounds was not " accompanied by the gloomy despondency " which now depresses me, and by a slow, " but sure progress, is conducting me to " death. Only two months ago, I was strong, " intrepid, capable of braving every fatigue:

"now, confined to this horrid abode, my
"courage is vanished, every thing forsakes
"me. I have, in vain, asked some assistance
"of those who have come to see me, not
"from humanity, but from unfeeling curio-
"sity: thus, people went to Liege to see
"the brave Goffin, after he had extricated
"himself by his courage, from the coal-pit
"which had fallen in and buried him. But
"he, happier than I, was rewarded with the
"cross of the legion of honour, and a pen-
"sion which enabled him to subsist.* If I

---

* The affair of the coal-mine of Beaujon, as a journalist has well observed, insures lasting celebrity to the name of the brave Goffin, whose memory the French Academy has consecrated by a poetical prize; and the city of Liege, by a large historical picture which has been publicly exhibited.—Doubtless the devotedness of Goffin was sublime; but, Goffin was only the victim of a natural accident, no sentiment of honour and duty, had plunged him voluntarily into an imminent danger, as it had many of those on the raft, and which, several of them might have avoided. Goffin, accusing only fate and the laws of nature, to which we are subject, in every situation, had not to defend his soul against all the odious and terrible impressions of all the unchained passions of the human heart: hatred, treachery, revenge, despair, fratricide, all the furies in short, did not hold up to him their hideous and threatening spectres; how great a difference does

"were in France," he continued, "my re-
"lations, my countrymen, would mitigate
"my sufferings; but here, under a burning
"climate, where every thing is strange to
"me, surrounded by these Africans, who
"are hardened by the habitual sight of
"the horrors produced by the slave trade,
"nothing relieves me; on the contrary, the
"length of the nights, the continuance of
"my sufferings, the sight of those of my
"companions in misfortune, the disgusting
"filth by which I am surrounded, the inat-
"tention of a soldier who acts as nurse, and
"is always drunk or negligent, the insup-
"portable hardness of a wretched bed, scarce-
"ly sheltered from the inclemency of the
"air, all announce to me an inevitable
"death. I must resign myself to it, and
"await it with courage! I was less to be

---

the nature of their sufferings, suppose in the souls of those who had to triumph over the latter? and yet, what a contrast in the results! Goffin was honored and with justice; the men shipwrecked on the raft, once proscribed, seem to be for ever forsaken. Whence is it that misfortune so perseveringly follows them? Is it that, when power has been once unjust, has no means to efface its injustice but to persist in it, no secret to repair its wrongs, but to aggravate them?

" pitied on the raft; then my imagination
" was exalted, and I scarcely enjoyed my
" intellectual faculties! but here, I am only
" an ordinary man, with all the weaknesses
" of humanity. My mind is continually
" absorbed in melancholy reflections; my
" soul sinks under incessant sufferings, and
" I daily see those who shared my unhappy
" fate, drop before me into the grave."*

While he was wholly absorbed in this distressing soliloquy, he saw two young officers enter the room, followed by three or four slaves, carrying various effects. These two officers approached, with an air of kindness, the mournful and motionless Corréard, " Accept," said they, " these trifling presents, they are sent to you by Major " Peddy, and Captain Cambpell:" we, sir, have desired the happiness of bringing you this first assistance; we were commissioned by all our comrades, to obtain from you accurate information respecting your wants; you are, besides, invited to partake of our

* Three men saved from the raft, died in a very short time; those who crossed the desert, being too weak to go to Deccard, were in considerable numbers in this same hospital, and perished there successively.

table, all the time we shall pass together; the Major, and all the officers, beg you to remain here, and not to go to the pestilential camp at Deccard, where a mortal distemper would carry you off in a few days." It would be ungrateful not to name these two young officers: one bears the name of Beurthonne, without being a relation of the Governors; the name of the other is Adam.

While these generous officers were fulfilling, with so much politeness and kindness, these acts of humanity, Major Peddy entered the room, followed by other slaves, also loaded with things, which he came to offer to the friend of the naturalist, Kummer, by whom he was accompanied. The Major approached the unfortunate Corréard, who seemed as if awaking from a dream; he embraced him, shedding tears, and vowing to him a friendship which never abated during the whole time that he remained with him. What a sublime image is a fine man, almost two metres in height, who sheds tears of pity at the sight of an unfortunate man, who was not less affected, and shed them in abundance, penetrated with the most delicious feelings of gratitude and admiration. After he had recovered from the emotion excited in him by the sight of the melancholy situation of the stranger, whom he had just snatched from misery, the Major made him the most obliging offers: and that Mr. Corréard might not decline them, he assured him, beforehand, that he himself and many of his comrades had received similar assistance from Frenchmen; and that their countrymen ought to allow him the honour of discharging, if it were possible, his debt to their nation, for the generous treatment which he had received from them.* Offers so nobly made, could not but be accepted by Mr. Corréard, who expressed to his benefactor, how happy he should esteem himself to be able to merit the friendship that he had just offered him, and that he wished nothing so much as to be able, one day, to

---

* Major Peddy had fought against the French in the Antilles and in Spain; the bravery of our soldiers, and the reception given him in France at the time of our disasters, had inspired him with the greatest veneration for our countrymen, who had, on more than one occasion, shewn themselves generous towards him.

shew his gratitude in a manner worthy of himself, and of a Frenchman. From that time Mr. Corréard received all imaginable assistance from the Major and his officers, and it may be said with truth, that he owes them his life, as do the four French officers who were with him.

On the 24th of August, Mr. Clairet paid the debt of nature. It was thirty-four days after our arrival at St. Louis. Mr. Corréard had the grief to see him die at his side, and to hear him say before his death, that he died satisfied, since he had had time to recommend to his father a natural son whom he loved. At this time Major Peddy had not yet relieved Mr. Corréard; he was without clothes, so that he could not attend the funeral of his comrade, who had just expired, worn out by the sufferings which he had experienced on the raft.

The remains of this young officer received the honours due to them. The English officers, and especially Major Peddy, acted on this occasion in a manner worthy of praise.

Perhaps our readers will not be sorry to be made acquainted with some of the details of this mournful ceremony. They are drawn up by Mr. Corréard, who still feels a sad pleasure in calling to mind the moments which necessarily made upon him so great an impression.

The body of the unfortunate Clairet was laid out in a subterraneous apartment of the hospital, whither immense crowds repaired to see once more the mortal remains of one who was almost regarded as an extraordinary man; and who, at this moment, owed to his cruel adventures, the powerful interest, which the public favor attached to him and to those, who had so miraculously escaped from all the combined afflictions sustained on the fatal raft.

"About four o'clock in the afternoon," says Mr. Corréard, "I heard the mournful "sounds of martial instruments under the "windows of the hospital. This was a "dreadful blow to me, not so much because "it warned me of the speedy fate which in- "fallibly awaited me, as because this funeral "signal announced to me the moment of "eternal separation from the companion of "my sufferings: from the friend, whom "our common misfortunes had given me,

"when I passed with him the most dread-
"ful moments of my life. At this sound I
"wrapped myself in my sheet, and crawled
"to the balcony of my window, to bid him
"the last farewell, and to follow him with
"my eyes as far as possible. I know not
"what effect the sight of me may have pro-
"duced, but when I now reflect upon it
"myself, I imagine that the people must
"have believed it was a spectre welcoming
"a corpse to the abode of the grave.

"As for me, notwithstanding my emo-
"tion, the sacrifice which I supposed I had
"made of my life, permitted me to contem-
"plate and to follow in detail the sad spec-
"tacle on which my almost extinguished
"eyes eagerly dwelt. I distinguished a
"crowd of slaves who had obtained permis-
"sion from their masters to be present at
"the ceremony. A body of English sol-
"diers was placed in a line; after them
"came two lines of French soldiers and
"sailors. Immediately after, four soldiers
"bore the coffin on their shoulders, after
"the manner of the ancients. A national
"flag covered it, and hung down to the
"ground; four officers, two French and

" two English, were placed at the angles,
" diagonally opposite, and supported the
" corners; on the coffin were laid the
" uniform and the arms of the young
" soldier, and the distinctive marks of his
" rank. On the right and left French officers
" of the army and navy, and all the officers
" of the administration, ranged in two files,
" formed the procession. The band of mu-
" sic was at their head: afterwards, came
" the English staff with the respectable
" Major Peddy at its head, and the corps
" of citizens, led by the mayor of the town;
" lastly, the officers of the regiment, and a
" detachment, commanded by one of them,
" closed the procession. Thus was con-
" ducted to his last repose, this other victim
" of the fatal raft, snatched in the flower of
" his age, from his friends and his country,
" by the most fatal death, and whose fine
" qualities and courage rendered him wor-
" thy of a less deplorable fate."

This brave officer, who was only twenty-eight years of age, had been eight years in the service; he had received the cross of the Legion of Honor at the *Champ de Mai*, as a reward for the services which he had performed at Talavera de la Reina, Sierra Morena, Saragossa, Montmiraill, Champaubert, and Montéreau; he was present, also, at the too deplorable day of Waterloo; he was then ensign-bearer of his regiment.

Such were the events that passed in the isle of St. Louis. The bad season, which, in these countries is so fatal to the Europeans, began to spread those numerous and dreadful maladies, which are so frequently accompanied by death. Let us now turn to the unhappy persons assembled in the camp at Daccard, not far from the village of that name, situated on the Peninsula of Cape Verd.

The French Governor, as we have already observed, being unable to enter into the possesssion of the colony, resolved to go and remain upon Cape Verd, which had been recognized to be the property of France. On the 26th of July the Argus brig, and a three-masted vessel belonging to Messrs. Potin and Durécur, took on board the remains of the crew of the Medusa, that is, the men who had landed near Portendick, and some persons from the raft: those whose health were the most impaired remained in the hospital at St. Louis. These two vessels set sail; the Governor embarked on board that with three masts, and they arrived in the Goree Roads at nightfall. The next day the men were removed to Cape Verd: several soldiers and sailors had already repaired to it; (these were those who had first crossed the desert:) the flute, *la Loire*, had conveyed them thither some days before, with the commander of the frigate. It had also landed the troops it had on board, consisting of a company of colonial soldiers. The command of the camp was confided to Mr. de Fonsain, a respectable old man, who died there the victim of his zeal. What procured him this fatal distinction was the resolution taken by the Governor to go and reside in the island of Goree, to be able to superintend the camp, and the ships, and doubtless for the sake of his health.*

---

* The Governor, who it seems did not like the sight of the unfortunate, had, however, no reason to fear that it would too much affect his sensibility. He had elevated himself above the little misfortunes of life, at least, when they did not affect himself, to a degree of impassibility, which would have done honor to the most austere stoic,

The shipwreck of the frigate having much reduced the number of the garrison, and occasioned the loss of a great quantity of provisions which she had on board, it was necessary to dispatch a vessel to France, to obtain assistance and fresh orders, on account of the difficulties that had been raised by the English Governor. The *Echo* corvette was chosen for this purpose, which sailed on the 29th of July, in the evening. She had on board fifty-five of those who

---

and which, doubtless, indicates the head of a statesman, in which superior interests, and the thought of the public good, leave no room for vulgar interests, for mean details, for care to be bestowed on the preservation of a wretched individual. Thus, when the death of some unhappy Frenchman was announced to him, this news no further disturbed his important meditations than to make him say to his secretary, " Write, that Mr such a one is " dead."

The governor is, at the bottom, doubtless, a man not destitute of sensibility; for example, he never passed by the king's picture (if any strangers were present) but he shed tears of emotion. But his great application to business, the numerous occupations, the divers enterprises which have agitated his life, have, if we may so express it, so long distracted his thoughts that he has at length felt the necessity of concentrating them wholly in himself.

We cannot here become the historians of the governor;

had been shipwrecked, three of whom were officers of the navy, the head surgeon, the accountant, three *élèves* of the marine, and an under surgeon. After a passage of thirty-four days, this corvette anchored in Brest Roads. Mr. Savigny says, that during the six years he has been in the navy, he has never seen a vessel so well kept, and where the duty was done with so much regularity as on board the Echo. Let us return to the new establishment, which collected the remnant of us on Cape Verd.

---

we do not know whether his modesty will ever permit him to publish the memoirs of his life; but the public who know, or easily may know, that having been an apothecary in Bengal, a physician in Madagascar, a dealer in small wares, and land-surveyor in Java, a shopkeeper's clerk in the isle of France and Holland, an engineer in the camp of Batavia, commandant at Guadaloupe, chief of a bureau at Paris, he has succeeded after passing through all these channels, in obtaining the orders of St. Louis, and the Legion of Honor, the rank of colonel, and the command of a colony; the public, we say, will reasonable conclude, that the governor is, without doubt, a universal man, and that it is very natural that so superior a genius should have set himself above many little weaknesses, which would have arrested his flight, and which are proper for none but weak minds, for good people who are made to creep on upon the common route, and to crawl on the ground.

A camp was formed there to receive them near a village inhabited by negroes, and called Daccard, as has been stated above. The natives of the country appeared to be pleased at seeing the French found an establishment on their coast. A few days after, the soldiers and sailors having had some misunderstanding, the latter were removed, and distributed between the Loire and the Argus.

The men who formed this camp were soon attacked with the diseases of the country. They were ill fed, and many of them had just endured long fatigues. Some fish, very bad rum, a little bread, or rice, such were their provisions. The chace also contributed to supply their wants; but the excursions which they made to procure game, frequently impaired their health. It was in the beginning of July that the bad season began to be felt. Cruel diseases attacked the unhappy French; who being exhausted by long privations, these terrible maladies spread with dreadful rapidity. Two thirds of them were attacked by putrid fevers, the rapid progress of which hardly allowed the physicians time, to administer that precious remedy, the produce of Peru, of which, by some mismanagement, the hospitals were nearly destitute.(22) It was in these distressing circumstances that Mr. de Chaumareys came to take the command of the camp. Other measures were taken, and the hospitals were no longer in want of bark; but dysenteries, which frequently proved mortal, spread every where. On all sides there were none but unhappy men who gave themselves up to despair, and who sighed after their country: it was scarcely possible to find men enough for the duty of the camp. It is remarkable, that the crews of the vessels, which were in the roads of Goree, were hardly sensible of the influence of the bad season: it is true these crews were better fed, better clothed, and sheltered from the inclemency of the air; it is, besides, pretty certain, that this road is healthy, while the maladies of the country prevail on shore. Such was the situation of the camp of Daccard, when, on the 20th of November, the French Governor, was authorized, by Mr. Macarty, Governor General of the English settlements, to inhabit, on the former coast of the French possessions, the place which should suit him the best. Mr. Schmalz chose St. Louis.*

As we were neither of us at the camp of Daccard, we have not been able to detail all that passed there, and to speak only of things, with which we are perfectly acquainted, we have been obliged to pass over this part of our narrative rather slightly.

Mr. Corréard, who had remained at the isle of St. Louis, hastened to pay his respects to the governor, when he came, in consequence of the permission of Mr. Macarty to inhabit that town. He relates, that on this occasion, the governor received him very well, pitied him much, and protested that if he had not been taken better care of, it was not his fault: Mr. Schmalz, allowed, that he had been the worst treated of all the shipwrecked persons, a thing which he had long known; " But, added he, your misfor-
" tunes are terminated, and henceforward
" you will want for nothing. I will send

---

* The giving up of the colony did not take place till six months after our shipwreck. It was not till the 25th of January, 1817, that we took possession of our settlements on the coast of Africa.

" you, every day, very good rations of rice,
" meat, good wine, and excellent bread;
" besides, in a short time, I will put you
" to board with Mr. Monbrun, where you
" will be extremely well off." These last promises were as unavailing as the first had been. One day, however, in a fit of the fever, Mr. Corréard sent his servant to the governor with a note, in which he asked for a bottle of wine, and one of brandy; he, in fact, received what he had asked for; but when he was recovered from his delirium, he was going to send back these two bottles; however, on reflection, he thought it would not be proper, and he resolved to keep them. This is all that he was able to obtain from the French authorities, during five month's time that he remained at Saint Louis. It is even probable that he would have returned to France without having cost his government the smallest trifle, but for that fit of the fever, which deprived him of his reason, and during which, he made the request which he afterwards thought to be indiscreet and improper.

On the 23rd, or 24th of November, he again saw his two benefactors Major Peddy and Captain Campbell, who were about to depart on their great expedition to the interior of Africa.

At the moment of their separation, Major Peddy was eager to give to Mr. Corréard the last marks of true friendship, not only by his inexhaustible generosity, but also by good advice, which the event has rendered very remarkable, and which, for this reason, we think it necessary to mention here. The following is pretty nearly the discourse which the good Major addressed to Mr. Corréard at their last interview: " Since your intention," said he, " is to
" return to France, allow me, first of all, to
" give you some advice; I am persuaded
" that, if you will follow it, you will one day
" have reason to congratulate yourself on
" it. I know mankind, and without pre-
" tending exactly to guess how your Mi-
" nister of the Marine will act towards
" you, I, nevertheless, think myself justi-
" fied in presuming that you will obtain
" no relief from him; for, remember that
" a minister, who has committed a fault,
" never will suffer it to be mentioned to
" him, nor the persons or things presented

" to him, that might remind him of his
" want of ability;* therefore, believe me, my
" friend; instead of taking the road to Paris,
" take that to London; there you will find

---

* What would our good Major have said if he had known that our Minister of the Marine, Mr. Dubouchage, had exposed himself in a far greater degree, to the embarrassment of the species of shame, attributed to him here, by confiding seven or eight expeditions to officers who do no more honour to his choice and discernment, than the expedition to Senegal has done.

Besides the Medusa, which was conducted so directly upon the bank of Arguin, by the Viscount de Chaumareys, Knight of St. Louis, and of the Legion of Honour, and in the intervals of his campaigns, receiver of the *droits réunis*, at Bellac, in Upper Vienne, every body knows that the Golo, bound from Toulon to Pondichery, nearly perished on the coast, by the unskilfulness of the Captain, Chevalier Amblard, Knight of St. Louis, and the Legion of Honour, who, in order not to lose sight of maritime affairs, had become a salt merchant, near Toulon...Neither is the *début* of the Viscount de Cheffontaine forgotten, who, on quitting Rochefort, whence he was to sail to the Isle of Bourbon, put into Plymouth to repair his masts, which he had lost after being three or four days at sea. Who does not know that it would be in our power to mention more examples of this kind?

We spare the French reader these recollections, which are always painful; besides, what could our weak voice add to the eloquent expressions which resounded in the last session, in the chamber of deputies; when a member,

" a number of philanthropits, who will
" assist you, and I can assure you that
" henceforward, you will want for nothing.
" Your misfortunes have been so very great

---

the friend of his country and of glory, pointed out the errors of the Minister of the Marine, and raised his voice against those *shadows of officers* whom favor elevated to the most important posts. He represented, with reason, how prejudicial it was to government, that the command of ships and colonies should be given as caprice dictates, and to gratify the pretentions of vain pride, while experienced officers were overlooked, or disdainfully repulsed, condemned to figure on the lists of the half-pay, of the *reforms*, and even before the time, which would have called them to a necessary, or at least legal repose. How burdensome to the State, are these *retraites* which render useless, men whose zeal and talents ought to insure no other than their vessel, who wished but to spend their life there in uninterrupted service, who would have found there a tomb, the only one worthy of a French sailor, rather than suffer any thing contrary to duty and honour. Instead of that, we have seen titles take the reward of knowledge, repose of experience, and protection of merit. Men proud of thirty years of obscurity, make them figure on the lists, as passed under imaginary colours, and this service of a novel description establishes for them the right of seniority. These men, decorated with ribbons of all colours, who counted very well the number of their ancestors, but of whom it would have been useless to ask an account of their studies, being called to superior commands, have not been able to shew anything but their

" that there is no Englishman who will
" not feel a pleasure in assisting you. Here,
" Sir, are 300 francs, which will suffice for
" the expences of your voyage, whether
" you go to Paris or to London. Reflect a
" moment on what I propose to you, and
" if your resolution is such as I wish you
" to take, let me know it immediately, that
" I may give you letters of recommendation
" to all my friends, as well as to my patrons,
" who will be truly happy to serve you."

Mr. Corréard was deeply affected by what he had just heard; the noble genero-

---

orders, and their unskilfulness. They have done more: they have had the privilege of losing the vessels and the people of the State, without its being possible for the laws to reach them; and after all, how could a tribunal have condemned them? They might have replied to their judges, that they had not passed their time in studying the regulations of the service, or the laws of the marine, and that, if they had failed, it was without knowledge or design. In fact, it would be difficult to suppose that they intended their own destruction; they have but too well proved that they knew how to provide for their own safety. And what reply could have been made to them, if they had confined their defence to these two points? We did not appoint ourselves; it is not we who are to blame.

sity of the excellent man to whom he already owed his life, and who entered with such perfect readiness, into all the details which he thought the most proper to finish his work, and insure the happiness of his poor friend, filled the heart of the latter with emotion and gratitude; yet, shall we say it? The advice to go to London, which the Major had just given him, had in it something that distressed him; he had not heard it without recollecting that he was a Frenchman, and some secret suggestions of self-love and national pride, told him that a Frenchman who had served his country, and to whom unparalleled misfortunes had given so many claims to the justice, as well as to the kindness of his own government, could not, without offering a kind of insult to his fellow countrymen, begin by going to England, and there throwing himself on the public compassion. These sentiments, therefore, suggested much more by his heart than by his understanding, dictated his answer to the Major.

It was not difficult for him to express, with warmth, all the gratitude which he owed him, for the noble and delicate manner in which he had sought him out, and relieved him in his misfortune.

"As for the pecuniary assistance which you still offer me," continued he, "I accept it with great pleasure, because benefits conferred by you, can only do honour to him who receives them, and because I hope, one day, to repay this debt with interest, to your countrymen, if I can meet with any who have need of my assistance. As for your other proposal, Major, allow me not to be of your opinion, and to have a little more confidence in the generosity of my government, as well as in that of my countrymen. If I acted otherwise, would you not be authorised to have a bad opinion of the French character, and then, I appeal to yourself, generous Englishman, should not I have lost my claims to your esteem? Believe me, Major, France can also boast of a great number of men, whose patriotism and humanity may rival those which are so frequently found in Great Britain. Like you we are formed to the sentiments, to the duties which compose the true love of our country and of li-

"berty. In returning to France, I firmly "believe that I return into the bosom of a "great family. But if, contrary to my ex- "pectation, it were possible that I should "find myself, one day, abandoned by my "government, as we were by some men "who have nothing French about them but "their dress; if France, which so often and "so nobly welcomes the unfortunate of "other countries, should refuse pity and "assistance to her own children, then, Ma- "jor, should I be obliged to seek, else- "where, a happier fate and a new country: "there is no doubt but that I should chuse "that of my generous benefactors in pre- "ference to every other."

Major Peddy answered Mr. Corréard only by tears. The transport of patriotism, in which the latter had naturally indulged himself, had found, as may be supposed, the heart of the noble Briton, in harmony with that of him whom he protected; he felt a visible satisfaction, and an emotion which he did not attempt to dissemble. The Major closely embraced Mr. Corréard, bidding him farewell for ever; it seemed that this worthy man forsesaw his approaching end.

He was in fact destined to sink beneath the fatigues of the journey which he was about to undertake.

This expedition was composed, besides the Major, who commanded in chief, and the Captain, who was the second in command, and charged with the astronomical observations, of a young Physician, who was third in command; of Mr. Kummer, the naturalist (a Saxon naturalized in France); of a Mulatto, who acted as interpreter; of thirty white soldiers, almost all workmen; of a hundred black soldiers, and of about ten camels, a hundred and fifty horses, as many asses, and a hundred oxen to carry burdens; so that there were above a hundred and thirty men, and four hundred animals. All the equipages were embarked on board six small vessels, which ascended the Rio Grande to the distance of about fifty leagues up the country. The respectable commander of this expedition could not resist the influence of the climate; he was attacked by a cruel disease, which terminated his existence a few days after his departure from the island of St.

Louis. Such men ought to be imperishable.*

---

* Just as we are going to send this sheet to the press, we learn from the newspapers, that this expedition has failed; that it was not able to proceed above fifty leagues into the interior, and that it returned to Sierra Leone, after having lost several officers, and among them Captain Campbell, who had taken the command after the death of Major Peddy. Thus the good fall and the Thersites live, and are often even honoured. Captain Campbell was one of our benefactors, may his manes be sensible to our regret, and may his family and country permit us to mingle with their just affliction, this weak tribute of respect, by which we endeavour as far as lies in our power to discharge the sacred debt of gratitude!

Among the losses which this expedition has experienced, it is feared that we must reckon that of our excellent companion, the Naturalist Kummer; nevertheless, as no possitive information of his death has yet been received of his fate, his numerous friends, in the midst of their fears, still cherish some hopes: May they not be disappointed.

The accounts which inform us of this event, attribute the ill success of the expedition, to the obstacles opposed to it by the natives of the interior, but enter into no details. We learn from geogaphers, that up the Rio Grande there lives the warlike nation of the Souucsous, whom some call the *Fonllahs* of Guinea. The name of their capital is Teembo. They are Mahometans, and make war on the idolatrous tribes who surround them, to sell their prisoners.

The English physicians finding that the health of Mr. Corréard far from improving, seemed on the contrary, to decline more and more, persuaded him to return to France. These gentlemen gave him a certificate of such a nature, that the French governor could not object to his departure; he received his request perfectly well, and two days after his passage was secured; but we shall see in the sequel what was the motive of this favorable attention to his request.

On the 28th of November, in the morning, he embarked on board of a coasting vessel, which conveyed him first on board the *Loire*, which was bound for France: he was no sooner embarked, than the fever seized him, as it did almost every day; he was in a dreadful situation, weakened by

---

A remarkable institution, called the *Pouarh*, seems to have a great resemblance with the ancient *secret Tribunal* of Germany. The *Pouarh* is composed of members who are not admitted among the initiated till they have undergone the most horrible probations. The association exercises the power of life and death; every body shuns him, whose head it has proscribed. It may be that it was by this species of government, which seems not to want power, that the English expedition was stopped.

five months' illness, consumed by a burning fever, added to the heat of the noon-day sun, which struck perpendicularly on his head; he thought he was going to die; he had, besides, painful vomitings, produced by the heat, and by an indisposition caused by the fish on which he had breakfasted before his departure. The little vessel crossed the bar; but it falling a dead calm, it could not proceed: they perceived this on board the *Loire*, and immediately dispatched a large boat to fetch the passengers out of the heat of the sun. While this boat was coming, Mr. Corréard fell asleep upon a coil of cables that were on the deck of the little vessel; but before he fell quite asleep, he heard some one say, "*There's one who will never get to France.*" The boat came in less than a quarter of an hour; all those who were about my sick friend, embarked on board the boat, without any one's having the generosity to awaken him; they left him asleep, exposed to the beams of the sun; he passed five hours in this situation, after the departure of the boat. In his life he had never suffered so much, except during the thirteen days on the raft. When he asked, on awaking, what was become of the other gentlemen, he was told that they were gone, and that not one of them had shewed any intention of taking him with them. A breeze springing up, his vessel at last reached the *Loire,* and there on the deck, in the presence of the sailors, he reproached in the bitterest manner, those who had abandoned him, and even said offensive things to them. These sallies, the consequence of his exasperation, caused him to be looked upon as out of his mind, and nobody troubled himself about the severe truths which he had thus publicly uttered. The *Loire* sailed on the 1st of December, and arrived in France on the 27th of the same month.

When Mr. Corréard got to Rochefort, he waited on the Intendant of the Marine, who received him kindly, and authorised him to remain in the hospital as long as he should think necessary for his recovery. He was placed in the officers' ward, where he received the utmost attention from the medical gentlemen, who besides the aid of their art, shewed him the greatest regard and mitigated his misfortunes by kind consolations. Mr. Savigny saw every day his companion in misfortune, and he often repeated, " I am happy, I have at length met " with men sensible to my misfortunes." After having passed thirty-three days in this fine hospital, he judged his health sufficiently recovered, and desired to leave it, in order to go to his family.

We shall here conclude the nautical part of our history; but as, since our return to France, particular circumstances and a series of events, which we were far from foreseeing, have, as it were prolonged the chain of our adventures, we think it will not be amiss to add another article, respecting what has happened to us since we have returned to our country.

Mr. Savigny thought, that after having undergone unexampled misfortunes, he had a right to describe all the sufferings to which he and his companions in misfortune had been exposed for thirteen days. Was it ever heard that the unhappy were forbidden to complain? Well, the fresh misfortunes which have befallen him, and which he is going to lay before our readers, have arisen, from his not having buried in silence these disastrous events.

During his passage on board the *Echo*, he wrote the account of our unhappy adventures; his intention was to deliver his narrative to the Minister of the Marine. When he arrived in France, in the month of September, some persons advised him to go to Paris, where, said they, " *Your misfor-* " *tunes will procure you the favor of* " *the Ministry,*" and it was considered as an absolute certainty, that some recompense would make him forget the considerable losses which he had sustained, the dangers which he had just escaped, and the pain arising from his wounds, for at that time he still wore his right arm in a sling. He listened to the advice which was given him, because it came from very sensible persons, and set out for the capital, carrying his manuscript with him. He arrived at Paris on the 11th of September; his first care was to go to the office of the Minister (of the Marine), where he deposited all the papers which he had drawn up respecting the shipwreck of the Medusa. But what was his astonishment to see the day after, the *Journal des Débats* of the 13th of September, an extract from his narrative, copied almost literally: he then endeavoured to discover whence the editors could have obtained these details; it cost him but little time to solve the riddle.

We shall not here explain by what means his manuscript became known to the editor of the *Journal*. We shall here content ourselves with saying, that while Mr. Savigny was still at Brest, a person, who has connexions with the officer of the marine, with the intention of serving him, asked him for a copy of his memoir, saying, that by the medium of a person in office, he could get it conveyed to the minister of the marine. This copy of our adventures was entrusted to this person, and by him sent to Paris. Mr. Savigny had acted in this manner, because his intention, at that time, was to go to his family, without passing through the capital. It appears that this copy was not discreetly kept, since it reached the editor of the *Journal des Débats*: certainly, he who received it from Brest, was very far from wishing to injure the author of the memoir.

If he had had the smallest idea of all the disagreeable consequences aising from the publicity which he gave to the narrative, by shewing it to several persons, he would have kept it more carefully, or at least, he would have delivered it immediately to the minister of the marine for whom it was intended. This publicity, by means of the *Journal*, drew upon Mr. Savigny the most serious remonstrances. The very same day he was sent for to the office; he was told that his excellency was discontented, and that, he must immediately prove, that he was innocent of the publication of our misfortunes, which affected all France, and excited a lively interest in the fate of the victims. But for Mr. Savigny, every thing was changed; instead of the interest, which his situation ought to inspire, he had called down upon himself the severity of the minister, and was to justify himself, for having dared to write that he had been very unfortunate, by the fault of others. The reception he met with at the office affected him so much, that but, for the advice of some persons, he would have resigned his commission at once. There was but one means to prove, that it was not he, who had given his narrative to the editor of the *Journal des Débats:* this was to obtain the certificate of the editor himself. Conscious of the truth, he went to him, and that honorable writer, without hesitation, did homage to the truth, by the following certificate.

" I certify that it is not from Mr. Sa
" vigny, that I have the details of the ship-
" wreck of the Medusa inserted in the
" journal of the 13th of September, 1816."

(Signed)——The Editor of the *Journal des Débats.*

This certificate was put into the hands of M. **** and by him presented to his excellency, who, however, did not appear satisfied, because this certificate, though it proved, that Mr. Savigny was not the person who had rendered public the history of our adventures, threw no light on the means by which the manuscript had become known to the editor. One of the principal persons in the office, having signified to him the opinion of his excellency, who found this justification insufficient, Mr. Savigny again had recourse to the editor of the journal, who gave a second certificate as follows.

"I certify, that it is not from Mr. Savigny, that I have the details inserted in the Number of the 13th of September, but from the office of the Minister of the Police." After this new proof, it was no longer doubted, but that Mr. Savigny had been the victim of an indiscretion, and he was told that he might return to his post. He therefore left the capital, after having experienced many vexations; but those, which the publication of our misfortunes was to cause him, were not yet at an end.

The English translated the details contained in the Journal of the 13th of September, and inserted them in one of their Journals which reached Senegal. In this amplified translation, there were some pretty strong passages, which were far from pleasing the governor, and M. * * * *, one of the officers of the frigate. They perceived that there was but one means to combat the narrative; this was to endeavour to make it believed, that it was false in many particulars. A report was therefore drawn up at St Louis; it was brought to Mr. Corréard to be signed, who, after perusing it, refused, because he found it contrary to the truth. The governor's secretary came several times to the hospital, to urge him for his signature; but he persisted in his refusal: the governor himself pressed him very earnestly one day that he went to solicit leave to depart; he answered, that he would never consent to sign a paper quite at variance with the truth, and returned to his hospital. The next day, his friend, Mr. Kummer, went to him, and invited him to return to the governor's, in order, at length, to sign this paper, because he had been informed, that if he persisted in his refusal, he should not return to France. These gentlemen, must therefore, have felt themselves deeply interested, to be reduced to employ such measures towards an unfortunate man, exhausted by a long sickness, and whose recovery depended on his return to Europe, which they thought not to grant him, except on condition of his signing a false narrative, contrary to what he had himself seen; for one paragraph was employed to prove that the towrope had *broken;* could he sign it, who was himself an eye witness, and who had been assured by more than twenty persons, that it had been *made loose*. Besides this falsehood, it was stated one passage, that, when the raft was left, the words *we abandon them*, were not pronounced; in another passage, that Mr. Savigny, in publishing his account, had shewn himself ungrateful to his officers, who had done every thing to serve him personally; there were, besides, some improper personalities: he was in particular much surprised to see at the bottom of this paper, the signature of a man, whose life Mr. Savigny had saved with his own hand.* Mr. Corréard's perseverance in

---

* This remark on the conduct of one of our companions whom we had known, under more favourable circumstances, had cost us some pain in the first edition: therefore, we did not expressly name the person meant. When we now name Mr. Griffon, we conceive ourselves to be fulfilling a duty, which his present sentiments impose on us.

A man of honor, especially, when in the state of weakness, and of mental and bodily infirmity to which we were reduced, might be misled for a moment; but when he repairs this involuntary error, with the generosity which dictated the following letter, we repeat it, there is no longer any crime in having thus erred, and it is justice, and a very pleasing duty for us to do homage to the frankness, to the loyalty of Mr. Griffon, and to congratulate ourselves, on having found again the heart of the companion of our

withholding his signature, triumphed over injustice, and his return to Europe was no longer retarded. But the same manœuvres

---

misfortunes, such as we had known him, and with all his rights to our esteem.

The following is the letter which he has just written to Mr. Savigny, and which is a highly valuable proof of the truth of our accounts.

Extract of a letter from Mr. Griffon to Mr. Savigny.

At present, Sir, I owe you a testimony of gratitude for your attention in anticipating me. I know, that in your eyes I could not merit so much generosity from you: it is noble to forget the ills that have been done us, and to do good to those who have sought to injure us: your conduct towards me is admirable; I confess, that, though my reclamations were just at the first, I have suffered myself to be carried too far by the first impulse of a weak and exalted imagination, which led me to decry my unhappy companion in misfortune, because I fancied, that the account which he had drawn up of our misfortunes might render us odious to all our relations and friends.** Such are the reasons which I alledged to you at Rochefort, and you must then have perceived, that I spoke to you with frankness, since I concealed nothing from you. I am not at present without repentance, for not having waited for better information, before I acted against one, whose firmness did not a little contribute to save our lives.

Bourgneuf, January 7, 1818. GRIFFON DUBELLAY.

** The same means were employed with Mr. Corréard.

had more success in another quarter, and Messrs. Dupont, Lheureux, Charlot, Jean Charles, and Touche-Lavilette could not escape the snare which was laid for them. They were labouring under that terrible fever which carried off the French with so much rapidity, when they were invited by the governor to sign this narrative. Some yielded to the fear of displeasing his excellency; others conceived hopes of obtaining his protection, which, in the colonies is no trifling advantage; others again were so weak, that they were not even able to make themselves acquainted with the paper to which they were desired to put their names. It was thus, that our companions were induced to give testimony against themselves, to certify the contrary of what they had seen respecting all that had been done, to bring about our destruction. Our readers have just seen the noble disavowal of Mr. Griffon, of the false impressions which had deceived him in respect to us: in order that the reader may be able to form a just opinion of the report directed against us, we insert here a document equally precise and decisive: it is a declaration of Mr. Touche-Lavillette, who acknowledges, that he signed in confidence, a paper, the contents of which were unknown to him, as well as the purpose for which it was drawn up.*

Thus supported by authorities, the value of which any body can now appreciate, this tardy and inexact report was

---

* I, the undersigned chief of the workmen under the command of Mr. Corréard, engineer, geographer, one of the members of the commission appointed by his excellency the minister of the marine and the colonies, to examine Cape Verd and its environs, certify that, in the month of November, 1816, a memorial was presented me to sign, by order of the governor of Senegal; that, at this time, living in the hospital in the island of Goree, to be cured of an epidemic fever, which then raged on Cape Verd; it occasioned temporary fits of delirium; that consequently, this weakening of my moral faculties, and even the state of mental derangement, in which I was caused to sign this piece without reading it: it appears, that it tended, in part, to blame the conduct of Mr. Savigny on the raft, and for which I owe him, only commendations. It appears, also, according to what has been told me, that I have been made to certify, that the tow-rope broke and was not loosened; I declare, that my signature at the bottom of this memorial, having been surreptitiously obtained, is null and void; in testimony whereof, I have delivered the present certificate to serve towards repelling any attack that might be made against Mr. Savigny, on the ground of this memorial.

Done at Paris, November 1, 1817. TOUCHE LAVILETTE.

addressed to the minister of the marine. Mr. Corréard, when he landed at Rochefort, informed Mr. Savigny of it, and gave him a certificate of what has been just related. The latter procured two others, which were delivered to him, by those of his companions in misfortune, who were in France. These certificates will be found in the notes. (1) (2) (3).

---

(1) I, the undersigned, appointed to command the raft of the Medusa frigate, certify, that Mr. Savigny, the surgeon, who embarked in the said raft, has given on all occasions, in the unhappy situation in which we were placed, proofs of the greatest courage and coolness, and that on several occasions, his prudence was of the greatest service to us, in suggesting to us means to maintain good order, and discipline, of which we had so much need, and which it was so difficult for us to obtain.

(Signed) COUDIN.

(2) I, the undersigned, certify, that Mr. Savigny, by his courage and coolness, succeded in maintaining good order upon the raft, and that, his prudent arrangements saved the lives of the fifteen unfortunate persons, who were taken up by the *Argus* brig.

(Signed) NICOLAS FRANÇOIS.

(3) I, the undersigned, certify, to all whom it may concern, that I have refused to sign a memorial drawn up by Mr.———, which was addressed to his excellency the minister of the marine, and tended to disapprove the con-

Provided with these three certificates, Mr. Savigny solicited permission to go to Paris, in order to be able to let his excellency see, that they were seeking to deceive him. Two months passed without information. Mean time, Mr. Corréard departed for the capital, taking a letter from his comrade, for a person in the office, to whom it was delivered, and who did not give a decisive answer to what was asked of him. At length, Mr. Savigny received a letter from Paris, in which he was informed, " That " not only he would not receive the permis- " sion which he solicited, but that, as long " as the present minister was at the head of " affairs, he would have no promotion." This letter, which he had so long expected, was dated May 10, 1817. Mr. Savigny disgusted by all that he had just experienced, gave in his resignation, after having served

---

duct of Mr. Savigny on board the raft, as well as to refute some parts of the narrative of our shipwreck, inserted in the *Journal des Débats*, the 13th of September, 1816, besides, the events related in this memorial, appear to me so entirely false, and so contrary to all that we owe to Mr. Savigny, that it was impossible for me to put my name to it. (Signed) CORRÉARD.

six years, and made as many expeditions by sea. On leaving the service, this medical officer, who had several times narrowly escaped perishing in the waves, was honored by the regret of the superiors under whom he has been employed, as may be judged by the copy of the* certificate, which they gave him when he resigned his situation. Fresh misfortunes have also befallen Mr. Corréard, from the time that he left Rochefort, till the moment that he was able to join his companion in misfortune, to write together the account of their shipwreck.

On the 4th of February 1817, thinking himself entirely recovered, he resolved to set out for Paris, where business rendered his presence necessary; but as his pecuniary resources were slender, and he had been

---

* The Board of Health certifies, that Mr. Jean Baptiste Henry Savigny, has been employed in the character of surgeon, from the 15th of April, 1811, to the 5th of May, 1817, and that in the course of his service, both by sea and land, he has given proofs of zeal, emulation, and good conduct.

It is with regret, that the Board of Health, sees an officer retire from the service, who is so distinguished by his talents as Mr. Savigny.

(Signed)   CHASLON, TUFFET, RÉJOU.

at considerable expence to clothe himself, (for he was almost naked when he landed from the *Loire*) he thought he could make the journey on foot. On the first day he felt only a slight pain, on the second it increased, and on the third, the fever seized him. He was then three leagues from Poitiers, near a very little village: exhausted with fatigue, and weakened by the fever, he resolved to go to the mayor, and ask him for a billet; this functionary was from home, but his wife said, that at all events, it would be necessary first to obtain the consent of Monsieur the Marquis de...... Colonel of the National Guard. The weary traveller thought there could be no impropriety in waiting on the Marquis: he was deceived in his expectation; the Colonel gave him a very bad reception, and was insensible to his entreaties; it was in vain that he shewed him his certificates, his pass, his wounds, and even his arms which shook with the fever: nothing could move him. The unfortunate invalid, in despair, retired, cursing the inhumanity, which he had not expected to find in an officer of the National Guard, promising in his own mind, never to forget his illustrious name, and the unfeeling manner in which he had answered to his requests. Exhausted as he was, he was obliged to drag on another weary league on foot, in order to reach a public house where he might rest himself. The next day, with much difficulty, he got to Poitiers. He had the happiness to find a man of feeling in the Mayor, who was much affected by his melancholy situation; it was, indeed, calculated to excite interest; for a few minutes before he entered the town-hall, he fainted, but the most charitable assistance was bestowed on him by a respectable lady, and he soon recovered from this swoon. One of the clerks soon gave him a billet, assuring him that it was upon one of the best houses in the town; which was true; and the poor invalid owns, that in his life, he never has received more affectionate care than that which he met with in the house of Mr. Maury, proprietor of the hotel of the Roman Antiquities. Poitiers was therefore a place of happiness for him. It was soon known in the town, that one of the shipwrecked persons from the raft, was within its walls; and during the whole day nothing was spoken of but that melancholy event. Two persons, well known for their talents, and the high offices which they have filled, came to the relief of Mr. Corréard: both had been formerly exiled; they knew what misfortune was, and knew how to pity that of an unhappy man, who had just experienced such extraordinary hardships; they invited him to spend the whole of the fine season at their country houses; but desiring to reach Paris as soon as possible, he refused the generous offer that was made him, and after having rested three days at Poitiers, he left it by the diligence, and at last arrived in the capital.

On his arrival, his first step was directed by gratitude; he recollected the signal services which he had received from the English officers, during his abode at Saint Louis; and his heart urged him to enquire of the ambassador of that nation, if he had not received any intelligence respecting his benefactors.*

---

* *To His Excellency the British Ambassador, at the Court of France.*

My Lord,

A Frenchman who, after a shipwreck without parallel,

After he had thus discharged the duty which was imposed on him by their beneficence, he made all the necessary applications to the office of the Marine to obtain an employment in the capital. He was answered that it was impossible, advising

---

has been fraternally assisted by foreigners whom national interests seemed calculated to estrange from him, is eager to give utterance to the sentiments of gratitude with which he is filled.

This Frenchman, My Lord, is Alexander Corréard, an engineer, an honorary member of the commission appointed to examine Cape Verd and its environs, one of the fifteen persons who escaped out of the hundred and fifty individuals shipwrecked, with the raft of the Medusa frigate, of whom only eleven are still living.

It is this want of my heart, which emboldens me to address Your Excellency, the worthy representative in my country of that of my generous benefactors, whose names will be ever memorable in the annals of humanity.

Yes, My Lord, it is a duty delightful to my heart, to declare, that the justest title to the gratitude of all the French has been acquired by Major Peddy, commanding the Expedition to the Interior of Africa, charged to continue the great undertaking of Mungo Park, by the obliging generosity which he shewed to the unfortunate men who escaped from the fatal raft, by bestowing on them linen, clothes, money and admitting them to his table, &c. These attentions were aided by Captain Campbell, the second in command, who never ceased to load me also with his benefits; in short, in imitation of them, all the English

him to make an application for a situation in the colonies, particularly Cayenne. Three months passed in useless solicitations to obtain this employment, as well as the decoration of the legion of honour, which he had been led to hope for.

During this time he neglected nothing

Officers, both those of the Expedition, as of the Royal African Regiment in garrison at St. Louis, vied with each other in relieving us, especially Captain Chemme, Lieutenant Hommera, Adjutant-Major Grey, Ensigns Beurthonne and Adams.

May Your Excellency receive with kindness, the sincere expression of gratitude to the English nation, of a French private citizen who has been ruined by this dreadful disaster. Above all, may what he has experienced give his countrymen fresh reason to esteem these brave officers, at the same time that it is a proof of the wisdom of a government, which, among so many enlightened persons, has so well chosen, to finish an immense enterprise, co-operators, whose distinguished talents and social virtues, must ensure success, which promises such great advantages to the universe.

Relying on Your Excellency's generosity, Mr. Corréard begs you to be pleased to transmit to him some information respecting his benefactors, and particularly the honorable Major Peddy, to whom he has vowed eternal attachment,

I have the honour to be, &c.

A. CORRÉARD.

Paris, March 5, 1817.

which he thought might conduce to enable him to attain the object which he thought he might propose to himself without being accused of extravagant pretensions. Excited by the advice of a great many persons, whose judgment, as well as their noble and generous sentiments, commanded implicit confidence, he resolved to go to the very fountain of favors, to carry into the royal palace the sight of his strange misfortune, to invoke that hereditary goodness, the bright patrimony of the Bourbons, which so many other unfortunate persons have not solicited in vain. But the malignant influence of the adverse star, which so long persecuted Mr. Corréard, doubtless continued to manifest itself here. Neither he nor any other person will accuse the heart of the august personages to whom he addressed his petition; but whether timidity, the natural concomitant of misfortune, or a certain delicacy, hindered him from renewing his applications, for fear of seeming importunate, whether, as in the crowd of solicitors who surround princes, it is morally impossible that some should not be forgotten or less remarked, Mr. Corréard's ill-fortune placed him among this less favored number, or whether it be the effect of some other unknown adverse cause, he obtained on this side only vain hopes, as well as a just idea of the obstacles of every kind, with which the best princes are, as it were, surrounded without being conscious of it, and which keep back or turn aside the favor, which is always granted in their heart, just at the moment that it is on the point of being declared.

He first presented a petition to His Royal Highness Monsieur. He solicited the insignia of that order which was instituted to recompence all kinds of civil and military merit, to spread among all classes of society, the noble flame of emulation, of that order which was offered to Goffin, whose firmness forced his desponding companions, to hope for the assistance that was preparing for them: which has just been given to several of the shipwrecked crew of *La Caravane,**

---

* The flute *La Caravane*, commanded by Mr. Le Normand de Kergrist, perished in the dreadful hurricane, which was experienced at Martinique and some other Islands, on the 21st and 22nd of October last. Messrs. Fournier Lieutenant, Legrandais, and Lespert Midship-

who in their disaster, shewed themselves equally generous and intrepid; but who, however, had nothing to complain of but the elements, nothing to combat but the tempest.

He has every reason to believe that Monsieur had the goodness to sign his petition; but he has not been able to discover where, or how it has been lost on the way without reaching its destination. In the inquiries which he made at the office of the Prince's Secretary, he met with a young man eighteen or 20 twenty years of age, who already wore the same mark of merit which Mr. Corréard desired, and who only expressed an astonishment which was more than disobliging, at the subject of his demand, asking him if he had been twenty-five years in the service. Mr. Corréard, feeling on his side something more than surprise, thought it best to withdraw, but not till he had observed to this very young man, that he who appeared so difficult about the claims of

---

man, and Paulin Boatswain, have received the cross of the Legion of Honor for their conduct on this occasion.—Vide the *Moniteur* of January 22.

others must, according to appearance, in order to obtain the cross of the legion of honor, have got the years of his ancestors services counted instead of his own.

His friends again persuaded him to petition the Duke d'Angouleme, from whom, as High-Admiral of France, these friends thought that Mr. Corréard might expect an intervention more likely to promote the success of his application to the Minister of the Marine. He therefore went to the Tuileries on the 8th of May, and though his wounds still rendered walking painful to him, he had the good fortune to meet with the Prince as he was coming from a review, and to present him a memorial as he passed. His Royal Highness received him graciously, expressed his satisfaction at seeing one of the persons who had escaped from the fatal raft, and pressing his hand in the most affable manner, said to him, " My friend, " you have experienced very great misfor- " tunes. It seems that amidst these disas- " ters you have behaved well." After having run over the memorial, the Prince was pleased to add: " Thus it is that the " King should be served; I will recom-

"mend you to His Majesty, and let him
"know your conduct and your situation."

These marks of kindness have hitherto been all that Mr. Corréard has obtained by this memorial. However, His Royal Highness transmitted it to the navy-office, but there is every reason to suppose that it will remain buried there amidst the mass of papers; from which it might be presumed that the recommendations of princes are received with great indifference by the clerks of ministers, and that their offices are the shoals where the petitions of the unhappy are lost; in fact, a man of great experience, to whom Mr. Corréard communicated this mischance, told him, that, in such an affair, he would rather have the protection of the meanest clerk, than that of the first prince of the blood.

We think it superfluous to detain the reader any longer, with two or three other attempts, which were still more unfortunate, and only revived painful recollections in the mind of Mr. Corréard.

At last he received a letter from the Minister of the Marine, dated the 4th of June: it was a thunder-clap to him, for he was made to understand that all his applications would probably be in vain.

However, on the 20th of July, he received a note from Mr. Jubelin, inviting him to call at the Office of the Marine. His heart opened at this ray of hope; it was merely to know whether it were true, that he had received a pass to repair from Rochefort to his home. He answered in the affimative, which seemed to cause much surprise, for one had just been refused to Mr. Richefort, who solicited it in vain, though he was also one of those shipwrecked. He profited by the opportunity to inquire whether the expedition to Cayenne was soon to depart? A vague answer being returned, he represented how unfortunate he and his companions on the raft were, that they could obtain nothing, while some officers of the frigate had been appointed to commands. Mr. Jubelin answered that the ministry owed them nothing, and particularly to him: that he had gone of his own free will, and had engaged to ask nothing of the minister, except what was stipulated and mentioned in the treaty of May 16, 1816, by which His Excellency made to the explorers, numerous concessions (which it would be too long to mention here) on condition that they should correspond with His Excellency, through the Governor of Senegal; that they should be placed under the orders of that governor, and that they should undertake nothing without his approbation.

The impartial public will judge if, after such conventions, and having allowances, and passes from the government, it was to be presumed that he, who had been thus treated, would be told that they owed him nothing, not even assistance.

He learned, in the office, that the counsellor of State, Baron de Portal, had the intention to obtain for him, the decoration of the Legion of Honor, and that, for this purpose, he had had a memorial drawn up in his favour: but the minister had written in the margin, "*I cannot lay this request be-*"*fore the King.*" Thus the voice of the unfortunate Corréard could not reach the throne; the minister would not permit it. Doubtless if His Majesty had been informed, that some unhappy Frenchmen, who had escaped from the raft of the Medusa, had long and in vain solicited his minister, his paternal goodness would have given them proofs of his justice and his benevolence. His kind hand which is extended even to the guilty, by conferring his favors upon us his faithful subjects, would have made us forget our misfortunes and our wounds; but no, an unfriendly power, between us and the throne, was an insuperable barrier, which stopped all our supplications.

Mr. Corréard persuaded of the inutility of making fresh applications, gave up for the present all farther solicitation for what he had so well deserved by his courage and his services. The change in the ministry has revived his hopes: a letter from that department informs him that his Excellency would willingly embrace an opportunity to serve him*.

A minister, when he is really so dis-

---

* Paris, Sept. 8, 1817.

Sir.—The Memorials which you addressed on the tenth of June last, to the King and to His Royal Highness the Duke of Angouleme, have been referred to my apartment. I have examined the Memorials, as well as the letters which you have written on the same subject to my prede-

posed, easily finds means to employ an unfortunate man who asks but little.

Such are the vexations which we have experienced since our return to France: now returned to the class of citizens, though reduced to inactivity, after having exhausted our resources in the service, disgusted, forgotten, we are not the less devoted to our country and our king. As Frenchmen, we know that we owe to them our fortune and our blood. It is with the sincere expression of these sentiments that we shall conclude the history of our adventures.

In fine, we think that the reader will not be sorry to have some notices concerning the French settlements on the coast of Africa. As they seemed to us very interesting, we shall examine, but briefly, the places themselves, and the advantages that might be derived from them.

---

cessors. If an opportunity should occur, in which I can serve you, I will readily embrace it.

Receive, Sir, the assurance of my perfect consideration.

The Minister Secretary of State of the Marine and Colonies. COUNT MOLÉ.

These details will be a happy digression from the sad accounts of our misfortunes, and as the object of them is of great public utility, they will not be out of their place at the conclusion of a work, in which, we have thought it our duty, less for our own interest, than that of the public service, to employ our humble efforts for the disclosure of the truth.

The part of the coast beginning at Cape Blanco, and extending to the arm of the river Senegal, called the *Marigot* of the Maringouins, is so very arid, that it is not fit for any kind of cultivation; but from that *Marigot*, to the mouth of the river Gambia, a space, which may be about a hundred leagues, in length, with a depth of about two hundred, we meet with a vast country, which geographers call *Senegambia*.

Let us remark, however, before we go any further, that, notwithstanding the sterility of this part of the coast, it is not without importance, on account of the rich produce of the sea which bathes it. *The agriculture of the waters* as a celebrated naturalist has said, offers too many advantages, for the places that are adapted to it, to pass unobserved: this part of the sea, known by the name of the Gulph of Arguin, is especially remarkable for the immense quantity of fish which visit it, at different seasons, or which continually frequent these shores. This gulph, included between Capes Blanco and Merick, and the coast of Zaara, on which, besides the isle of Arguin which was formerly occupied, there are several others at the mouth of what is called the river St. John, is as it were closed towards the west, in its whole extent, by the bank which bears its name. This bank, by breaking the fury of the waves, raised by the winds of the ocean, contributes by securing the usual tranquillity of its waters, to render it a retreat for the fish, at the same time that it also favors the fishermen. In fact, it is from this gulph, that all the fish are procured which are salted by the inhabitants of the Canaries, and which constitute their principal food. They come hither every spring in vessels of about 100 tons burden, manned by 30 or 40 men, and they complete their operations with such rapidity, that they seldom employ more than a month. The fishermen of Marseilles and Bayonne might attempt this fishery. In short, whatever advantage may be sought to be derived from this gulph, so rich in fish, it may be considered as the African Bank of Newfoundland, which may one day contribute to supply the settlements of Senegambia, if the Europeans should ever succeed in establishing them to any extent. Among the species of fish found in this gulph, there is one, which seems peculiar to itself; it is that, which was caught on board the Medusa, and is the principal object of the fishery in these seas. An accurate description had been made of it, and Mr. Kummer made an exact drawing of it; but all was lost with the frigate. All that can be recollected of this description, is, that these fish which are from two to three feet long, are of the genus *Gade* or *Morue* (cod); that they do not appertain to any of the species mentioned by Mr. Lacépède, and that they belong to the section in which the *Merlan* is placed.

Whence comes the name of Arguin? who gave it to this gulph? If we consider the heat of the sun which is experienced here, and the sparkling of the sandy downs which compose the coast, we cannot help remarking that *Arguia* in Phenician means what is *luminous* and *brilliant*, and that in Celtic, *Guin* signifies *ardent*. If this name comes from the Carthaginians, who may have frequented these coasts, they must have been particularly struck with their resemblance to the famous Syrtes in their own neighourhood, which mariners took so much care to avoid.

Exercitas aut petit Syrtes Noto.

Some division of territory, or of pasturage among the hordes of the desert, was doubtless the cause, that the Europeans, who desired to carry on the gum trade, formerly chose the dangerous bay of Portendic, surrounded by a vast amphitheatre of burning sands, in preference to Cape Merick. Perhaps, the Trasas of the west, could not advance to the north of this bay, without quarrelling with the other Moors, who frequent Cape Blanco. This Cape Merick seems preferrable for commerce, either as a factory, to trade with the Moors, or as a place of protection for the traders, and the fishery. Its elevation and nature, afford a facility of defence, which is not found at Portendic; where there is not at present the smallest appearance of vegetation.

The Estuary of the river, St. John, at the back of this Cape, is now entirely destitute of verdure, and humidity, and salt is abundant in the neighbourhood.

But, as we have said above, it is when we penetrate a little into the interior, that an immense country, rich in the gifts of nature, invites European cultivation, and offers the fairest prospect of success for the colonial productions.

The soil is in general good, and all colonists from the Antilles, who have visited these countries, think that they are well adapted to the cultivation of all kinds of colonial produce. This immense country is watered by the Senegal and the Gambia, which bound it to the north and south. The river Falémé crosses it in the eastern part, as well as many other less considerable rivers, which, flowing in different directions, water principally that part covered with mountains which is called the high country, or the country of Galam. All these little rivers fall at length into the two large ones, of which we have spoken above.

These countries are very thickly peopled, and are in general mild and hospitable. Their villages are so numerous, that it is almost impossible to go two leagues without meeting with some, that are very extensive and very populous. Nevertheless, we have no more than two settlements; those of St. Louis and Goree; the others, which were seven or eight in number, have been abandoned; either, because the French and the English, who have occupied them in turn, have wished to concentrate the trade in the two settlements which still exist; or because the natives no longer found the same advantage in bringing their goods and slaves. It is, however, true, (as we have been assured) that in consequence of the abolition of those factories, the considerable commerce which France carried on upon this coast before the revolution, has been reduced to one fourth of its former extent. (23)

The town of St. Louis, the seat of the general government, is situated in longitude 18° 48′ 15″ and in latitude 16° 4′ 10″. It is built on a little island formed by the river

Senegal, and is only two leagues distant from the new bar formed by the inundation of 1812. Its situation in a military point of view, is pretty advantageous, and if art added something to nature, there is no doubt, but this town might be rendered almost impregnable; but in its present state, it can hardly be considered as any thing more than an open town, which four hundred resolute men, well commanded, might easily carry. At the mouth of the river is a bar, which is its strongest bulwark. It may even be said, that it would be impossible to pass it, if it were well guarded; but the coast of the point of Barbary, which separates the river from the sea is accessible; it would be even possible, without meeting with many obstacles, and with the help of flat bottomed boats, to land troops and artillery upon it. When this landing is once made, the place may be attacked on the side of the north, which is entirely destitute of fortifications. There is no doubt, but that, if it were attacked in this manner, it would be forced to surrender at the first summons. However, many have hitherto considered it as impregnable, believing that it was impossible to make a landing on the coast of Barbary, but as we are convinced of the contray, because the English already executed this manœuvre at the last capture of this place, we venture to call the attention of the government to the situation of St. Louis, which would certertainly become impregnable if some new works were erected on different points.

This town has, in other respects, nothing very interesting in it, only the streets are strait, and pretty broad, the houses tolerably well built and airy. The soil is a burning sand, which produces but few vegetables: there are only eight or ten little gardens, containing from two to four *ares* of ground at the most, all cultivated, and in which, within these few years orange and lemon trees have been planted, so that there is reason to suppose, that, with some care, these trees would thrive perfectly well. Mr. Corréard saw a fig-tree and an European vine, which are magnificent, and bear a large quantity of fruit. Since the colony has been restored to the French, several kinds of fruit-trees have been planted, which thrive in an extraordinary manner. Five or six *palatuviers*, and a dozen palm trees are dispersed about the town.

The parade is tolerably handsome; it is situated opposite the castle, and what is called the fort and the barracks. On the west it is covered by a battery of ten or twelve twenty-four pounders, and two mortars; this is the principal strength of the island. On the east is the port, where vessels lie in great safety. The population of the town amounts to 10,000 souls, as the Mayor told Mr. Corréard. The inhabitants of the island are both Catholics and Mahometans; but the latter are the most numerous, notwithstanding this, all the inhabitants live in peace and the most perfect harmony. There are no dissentions about religious opinions: every one prays to God in his own manner; but it is observed, that the men who have abjured Mahometanism, still retain the custom of having several wives. We think that it would not be very difficult to abolish it among the blacks, who are struck with the pomp of our religious ceremonies: they would be much more inclined to the Catholic religion, if it tolerated polygamy, a habit which will inevitably render all the efforts of the Missionaries abortive, as long as they commence their instruction by requiring its abolition.

The isle of St. Louis, by its important position, may command the whole river, being placed at the head of an Archipelago of pretty considerable islands: its extent is however small. Its length is 2,500 metres from north to south; and its breadth from east to west is, at the north part, 370 metres; in the middle of its length 28 metres; and at the south only 170 metres. The elevation of its soil is not more than 50 centimetres above the level of the river: in the middle it is however a little higher, which facilitates the running of the waters. The river dividing to form the isle of St. Louis has two arms, which reunite below the island: the principal situated on the east is about 1000 metres in breadth, and that on the west about 600. The currents are very rapid, and carry with them quantities of sand, which the sea throws back towards the coast; this it is that forms a bar at the mouth of the river; but the currents have opened themselves a passage, which is called the *pass of the bar.* This pass is about 200 metres broad and five or six metres in depth. Very often these dimensions are less; but at all times only such vessels can pass over it as draw four metres water at the utmost: the overplus is very necessary for the pitching of the vessel, which is always very considerable upon this bar. The waves which cover it are very large and short; when the weather is bad, they break furiously, and intimidate the most intrepid mariners.

The western arm of the river is separated from the sea by a point called the *Point of Barbary.* It is inconceivable how this slip of land, which is not above 250 metres in its greatest breadth, and is formed only of sand, should be able to resist the efforts of the river, which always tends to destroy it; and those of the sea, which breaks upon it sometimes with such fury, that it covers it entirely, and even crossing the arm of the river, comes and breaks on the shore of the island of St. Louis. Almost opposite the château and on the Point of Barbary, is a little battery of six guns at the most, which is called the *Fort of Guetander;* it is on the summit of a hill of sand which has been formed by the wind, and increases daily; it is even already pretty high, and is surrounded by a great number of huts of the blacks, which form a pretty extensive village: these huts tend to hold the sand together, and to prevent its sinking. The inhabitants of this village are very superstitious, as the following anecdote will prove.

In the course of the month of September, Messrs. Kummer and Corréard crossed the arm of the river, to visit the coast of Barbary and the village of Guetander; when they landed on the point, they proceeded towards the north, and having gone three or four hundred paces along the shore, they found a turtle, the diameter of which was a metre at the least; it was turned upon its back and covered with a prodigious quantity of crabs, (*toulouroux*)* which are found along the sea-coast. Mr. Corréard stopped a moment, and remarked that, when he had wounded one of

---

* A kind of crab found on the sea-coast; it is the *Cancer cursor* of Linnæus, and the same that is found on the shores of the Antilles.

these animals with his cane, the others devoured it instantly. While he was looking at these crabs feeding on the turtle, Mr. Kummer went on towards the south, and visited the burying-places of the blacks. Mr. Corréard joined him, and they saw that the natives erect over the tombs of their fathers, their relations and friends, little sepulchres, some made of straw, some of slight pieces of wood, and even of bones. All these frail monuments are consecrated much more by gratitude than by vanity. The blacks prohibit all approach to them in the strictest manner. Mr. Kummer, whom his companion had left to return to the shore, was examining very tranquilly these rustic tombs, when suddenly one of the Africans armed with a sabre, advanced towards him, crouching and endeavouring to surprise him; Mr. Kummer had no doubt but this man had a design upon his life, and retired towards Mr. Corréard, whom he found again observing the crabs and the turtle. On relating to him what had just passed, as they were unarmed, they resolved immediately to pass the river, by throwing themselves into a boat; they had soon reason to congratulate themselves on having done so, for they perceived several men who had collected at the cries of the black, and, if they had not taken flight, it is probable that their innocent curiosity would have cost them their lives.

The left bank of the river, which is called Grande Terre, is covered with perpetual verdure, the soil is fertile, and wants only hands to cultivate it.

Opposite, and to the east of St. Louis, is the isle of Sor, which is four or five leagues in circumference; it is of a long and almost triangular form: there are two extensive plains in it, where habitations might be erected. They are covered with grass two metres in height, a certain proof of the advantages that might be derived from the cultivation of this island. Cotton and indigo grow there naturally, the ground is in some parts low and damp, which gives reason to suppose that the sugar-cane would succeed. It might be secured against the inundations which take place in the rainy season, by erecting little causeways a metre in height, at the most. There are in this island, principally on the east side, mangoes, *palatuviers*, a great quantity of gum trees, or mimosas, and magnificent Baobabs*.

Let us stop for a moment before this colossus, which, by the enormous diameter to which it attains, has acquired the title of the *Elephant of the vegetable kingdom*. The Baobab often serves the negroes for a dwell-

---

* The Baobab or Adansoia of botanists, is placed in the class Monadelphia polyandria, in the family of malvaceous plants, and has but one species. The first of these trees seen by Adanson, were twenty-seven feet in diameter, about eighty-three feet in circumference. Ray says they have been seen thirty feet in diameter, and Goldberry says he saw one of thirty-four feet. According to the calculations of Adanson, a tree, twenty-five feet in diameter, must have taken 3750 years to acquire these dimensions, which would allow a foot growth in 150 years, or an in inch in twelve years and a half; but an observation of Goldberry's would quite overturn this calculation. He, in fact, measured a Baobab thirty-six years after Adanson, and found its diameter increased by only eight lines. The growth is not therefore uniformly progressive, and must become slower at a certain period of the age of this tree, in a proportion which it is hardly possible to determine. Otherwise, if we admitted that it takes thirty-six years to increase in diameter only eight lines, it would require fifty-four years for an inch, and 648 for a foot, which would make 16,200 years for a tree twenty-four feet in diameter!

ing, the construction of which costs no further trouble than cutting an opening in the side to serve as a door, and taking out the very soft pith which fills the inside of the trunk. The tree, far from being injured by this operation, seems even to derive more vigour from the fire which is lighted in it for the purpose of drying the sap, by carbonising it. In this state it almost always happens, that the bark, instead of forming a ridge at the edge of the wound, as happens with some trees in Europe, continues to grow, and at length covers the whole inside of the tree, generally without any wrinkles, and thus presents the astonishing spectacle of an immense tree recompleated in its organisation, but having the form of an enormous hollow cylinder, or rather of a vast arborescent wall bent into a circular form, and having its sides sufficiently wide asunder to let you enter into the space which it encloses. If casting our eyes on the immense dome of verdure which forms the summit of this rural palace, we see a swarm of birds adorned with the richest colours, sporting in its foliage, such as rollers with a sky-blue plumage, *senegallis*, of a crimson colour, souï-mangas shining with gold and azure; if, advancing under the vault we find flowers of dazzling whiteness hanging on every side, and if, in the center of this retreat, an old man and his family, a young mother and her children meet the eye, what a crowd of delicious ideas is aroused in this moment? Who would not be astonished at the generous fore-sight of nature? and where is the man who would not be transported with indignation if, while he was contemplating this charming scene, he beheld a party of ferocious Moors violate this peaceful asylum, and carry off some of the members of a family, to deliver them up to slavery? It would require the pencil of the author of the Indian Cottage, to do justice to such a picture.

This is not the only service which the blacks, who inhabit Senegambia, derive from the Adansonia or Baobab. They convert its leaves, when dried, into a powder which they call *Lalo*, and use it as seasoning to almost all their food. They employ the roots as a purgative; they drink the warm infusion of its gummy bark, as a remedy for disorders in the breast; they lessen the inflamation of the cutaneous eruptions, to which they are subject by applying to the diseased parts cataplasms made of the parenchyma of the trunk: they make an astringent beverage of the pulp of its fruit; they regale themselves with its almonds, they smoke the calyx of its flowers instead of tobacco; and often by dividing into two parts the globulous capsules, and leaving the long woody stalk fixed to one of the halves, which become dry and hard, they make a large spoon or ladle.

It has been found that the substance, called very improperly, *terra sigillata of lemnos*, is nothing more than the powder made of the pulp of the fruit of the Baobab. The Mandingians and the Moors carry this fruit as an article of commerce into various parts of Africa, particularly Egypt; hence, it finds its way to the Levant. There it is that this pulp is reduced to powder, and reaches us by the way of trade. Its nature was long mistaken: Prosper Alpinus was the first who discovered that it was a vegetable substance.

After the Isle of Sor, towards the South is that of Babagué, separated from the former and that of Safal, by two small arms of the river; this island, in an agricultural point of view, already affords a happy result to the colonists, who have renounced the inhuman traffic in slaves, to become peaceable planters. Many have already made plantations of cotton, which they call lougans. Mr. Artique, a merchant, has hitherto been the most successful. His little plantation brought him in 2400 fr. in 1814, which has excited in many inhabitants of St. Louis a desire to cultivate pieces of land there. After his example, we now see every where beginnings of plantations, which already promise valuable crops to those who have undertaken the cultivation of these colonial productions. The soil of Babagué is more elevated than that of the surrounding islands. At its southern extremity, which is precisely opposite the new bar of the river, there is a very great number of huts of the blacks, a military post with an observatory, and two or three country houses.

The Isle of Safal, belonging to Mr. Picard, offers the same advantages. Its soil is fertile as that of the islands of which we have just spoken. No drinkable water is found in any of them; but it would be easy to procure excellent water by digging wells about two metres in depth.

Cotton and indigo grow every where spontaneously; what then is wanting, to these countries, to obtain in them what the other colonies produce? Nothing but some men, capable of directing the natives in their labours, and of procuring them the agricultural implements, and the plants of which they stand in need. When these men are found, we shall soon see numerous habitations arise on the banks of this river, which will rival those in the Antilles. The blacks love the French nation more than any other, and it would be easy to direct their minds to agriculture. A little adventure, which happened to Mr. Corréard, will shew to what a degree they love the French.

In the course of the month of September, his fever having left him for some days, he was invited by Mr. François Valentin, to join a hunting party in the environs of the village of Gandiolle, situated six leagues to the South, South East of St. Louis. Mr. Dupin, supercargo of a vessel from Bordeaux, who was then at Senegal, and Mr. Yonne, brother of Mr. Valentin, were of the party. Their intention was to prolong the pleasures of the chace, for several days; in consequence, they borrowed a tent of the worthy Major Peddy, and fixed themselves on the banks of the gulph which the Senegal forms, since its ancient mouth is entirely stopped up, and a new one formed, three or four leagues higher up than the former. There they were only a short league from the village of Gandiolle. Mr. Corréard directed his course, or rather his *reconnaissances*, a little into the interior, for he had conceived the idea of taking a plan of the coast, and of the islands formed by the Senegal. He was soon near to Gandiolle, and stopped some moments at the sight of an enormous Baobob tree, the whiteness of which much surprised him: he perceived it was covered with a cloud of the birds called aigrettes.* He advanced across the village to the foot of this tree, and fired two shot successively, supposing he should kill at least twenty of

---

* These aigrettes or white herons, are found in large flocks in this part of Africa; they follow the cattle to feed on the insects with which they are infested.

these birds. Curiosity induced him to measure the prodigious tree, on which they were perched, and he found that its circumference was 28 metres. While he was examining this monstrous production of the vegetable kingdom, the report of his piece had caused a great many blacks to come out of their huts, who advanced towards Mr. Corréard, doubtless, with the hope of obtaining from him some powder, ball, or tobacco. While he was loading his piece, he fixed his eyes upon an old man, whose respectable look announced a good disposition; his beard and hair were white, and his stature colossal; he called himself Sambadurand. When he saw Mr. Corréard looking at him attentively, he advanced towards him, and asked him if he was an Englishman? No, replied he, I am a Frenchman. —How, my friend, you are a Frenchman! that gives me pleasure.—Yes, good old man, I am.—Then the black tried to put on a certain air of dignity to pronounce the word Frenchman, and said, " Your nation is the " most powerful in Europe, by its courage and the superiority of its genius, is it not?" —Yes.— It is true that you Frenchmen are not like the white men of other nations of Europe whom I have seen; that does not surprise me; and then, you are all fire, and as good tempered as we blacks. I think you resemble Durand in vivacity and stature; you must be as good as he was; are you his relation?—No, good old man, I am not his relation; but I have often heard speak of him.—Ah! you do not know him as I do: it is now thirty years since he came into this country with his friend Rubault, who was going to Galam. This Frenchman, whose language I learned at St. Louis, loaded us all with presents; I still keep a little dagger which he gave me, and I assure you that my son will keep it as long as I have done. We always remember those white men who have done us good, particularly the French whom we love very much.—" Well," answered Mr. Corréard, " I am sorry I have nothing which can suit you, and be kept for a long time, or I would offer it you with pleasure, and you would join the remembrance of me with that of the philanthropic Durand, who had conceived plans which, if they had been executed, would, perhaps, have been the glory of my country, and the happiness of yours; but here, take my powder and ball, if that can do you pleasure."—Ah! good Frenchman, I would willingly take them, for I know that you have as much as you please in your own country;* but at this moment it would deprive you of the pleasure of the chace.—No, take it all.—Take my advice Toubabe: let us divide it, that will be better. In fact, they divided. The black invited Mr. Corréard to enter his hut to refresh himself. " Come Toubabe," said he, " come, my women shall give you some milk and millet flour, and you shall smoke a pipe with me."

Mr. Corréard refused, in order to continue his sport, which was interrupted by the cries of the blacks, who pursued a young lion, which came from the village of Mouit, and attempted to enter that of Gandiolle; this animal had done no harm, but the natives pursued him in the hopes of killing him, and to sell his skin. Dinner time being come, all the white hunters returned to their tent. A few moments after, they saw a

---

* The blacks think that all the whites are very rich in their own country.

young negro, twelve years of age at the most, whose mild and pleasant countenance was far from indicating the courage and the strength which he had just displayed; he held in his hands an enormous lizard quite alive, at least a metre and eighty centimetres in length. These gentlemen were astonished to see this child holding such a terrible animal, which opened a frightful pair of jaws. Mr. Corréard begged Mr. Valentin to ask him how he had been able to take, and pinion it in this manner. The child answered as follows in the Yoloffe language: " I saw this lizard come out of a hedge, I immediately seized it by the tail and hind feet: I raised it from the ground, and with my left hand took it by the neck; and holding it very fast, and at a distance from my body, I carried it in this manner to the village of Gandiolle, where I met one of my companions, who tied his legs, and persuaded me to come and present it to the Toubabes who are in the tent; he told me also that they were Frenchmen, and as we love them much, I have come to see them, and offer them this lizard." After these details, Mr. Corréard presented the but end of his piece to the animal, which made a deep indenture with its teeth; having then presented it the end of the barrel, it immediately seized it furiously, and broke all its teeth, which made it bleed very much; nevertheless, it made no effort to disengage itself from its bonds.*

The environs of Gandiolle appear to be extremely fertile; we find there grass two metres in height, fields of maize and millet. This country is full of large pieces of water, which the natives call marigots; the major part of which cover an immense space; but it would be easy to drain them by means of some little canals, particularly in the part near the coast. These lands would be very productive, and proper for the culture of the sugar cane: the soil is mud mixed with very fine sand.(24)

---

* This lizard was probably a turpinambis. This animal, which is not uncommon at Cape Verd, climbs up trees, frequents the marshy places, and is said to inflict severe wounds if it is not laid hold of with great precaution. The inhabitants of the *Mamelles* assert that it devours young crocodiles. This species seems to be the same as that which frequents the banks of the Nile. It grows to the length of four feet and uses its tail in swimming.

After having examined the environs of St. Louis, let us cast a glance upon the rock called the Island of Goree, and its environs. This isle is nothing of itself; but its position renders it of the greatest importance; it is situated in longitude 19° 5′, and in latitude 14° 40′ 10″, half a league from the main land, and thirty-six leagues from the mouth of the Senegal. The Cape de Verd Islands, are eighty leagues to the West. It is this position that renders it mistress of all the commerce of these countries. Its port is excellent; and so great a number of ships and boats are seen there that its road is continually covered; there is so much activity that some persons have said the Island of Goree was, perhaps, the point in the world, where there was most bustle and population. The number of its inhabitants is estimated at 5000 souls, which is by no means in proportion with its confined surface, which is not above 910 metres in length, and 245 in breadth. Its circumference is not above 2000 metres. It is only a very high rock, the access to the coasts, of which is very difficult. The numerous rocks, which surround it on all sides, have made some navigators give it the name of *Little Gibraltar;* and if nature were seconded by art, there is no doubt but like that, it would become impregnable. It was first taken possession of by Admiral d'Estrées, about the end of the year 1677. This isle lies in the direction of S.S.E and N.N.W. and is only about 2500 metres distant from Cape Verd. It is defended by a fort, and by some small batteries in very bad condition; but it is, nevertheless, impregnable by its position. In fact, it is not accessible, except on the E.N.E. where there is a pretty large and deep bay, capable of receiving the largest ships. Its road is immense; vessels are safe in it, and tolerably well sheltered. At two leagues from Goree is the bay of Ben, which affords the greatest facilities for the careening of vessels, and for the repairs of which they may stand in need.

The Island of Goree is cool during the evening, the night and the morning; but during the day, there prevails in the island an unsupportable heat, produced by the reflection of the sun's rays, which fall perpendicularly on the Basalt rocks which surround it. If we add to this the stagnation of the air, the circulation of which is interrupted by the houses, being very closely built, a considerable population, which continually fills the streets, and is beyond all proportion with the extent of the town, it will be readily conceived that all these reasons, powerfully contribute to concentrate here such insupportable heat, that one can scarcely breathe at noon day. The blacks too, who certainly know what hot countries are, find the heat excessive, and prefer living at St. Louis.

The Island of Goree may become of the greatest importance if the government should ever think proper to establish a powerful colony, from Cape Verd to the river Gambia; then this isle would be the bulwark of the settlements on the coast of Africa. But it will be objected that Goree is very small, and that great establishments can never be formed there; we think, only, that it is proper to be the central point, till a greater colony shall be established on Cape Verd, which nature seems to have intended for it, and the advantages of which, in a military and maritime point of view, are of the highest importance. Men of sound judgment who have examined it, have considered it calculated to become one day a second Cape of Good Hope. It is certain that, with time and by means of some works, this Cape would become highly interesting, and would serve as a *dépôt*, to accustom to the climate, such Europeans, as might wish to settle either in the projected colonies, or on those which might be founded, between this Cape and the Gambia, or on the islands of Todde, Reffo, Morphil, Bilbas, and even in the kingdom of Galam.

The position and figure of Cape Verd are such, that it would be easy to form there an excellent port at a small expense; perhaps it would not be impossible to make some use of the Lake or *Marigot* of Ben, which is but a short distance from the sea. Its road, which is the same as that of Goree, might almost serve as a port, even in its present state. The following is an extract from a Letter, written to Mr. Corréard by a Physician, who has carefully examined Cape Verd.

" This Cape is very different from what
" we thought. Its surface is not above six
" or eight square leagues; its population is

" very numerous, and by no means in pro-
" portion with the part of this peninsula,
" proper for cultivation, which is not above
" one-third of its surface. Another third
" serves for pasture for the flocks of the
" blacks; and the other part is too much
" *vulcanised,* too full of rocks, to afford any
" hope of advantage in an agricultural
" view. But its military position is admir-
" able; all seems to concur to render it im-
" pregnable, and it would even be easy to
" insulate it entirely from the Continent,
" and to form upon it several ports, which
" nature seems to have already prepared."

This letter likewise speaks of the advantages offered by the environs of Rufisque, which are so well known, that we may dispense with speaking of them here. We shall only mention as among the principal points to be occupied, with the *mornes* of Cape Rouge, Portudal, Joal, and Cahone, this last on the river Salum near the Gambia; they are large villages, the environs of which are covered with magnificent forests, and the soil of which is perhaps the most fertile of any in Africa. For more ample accounts of these countries, we refer to the excellent works of Messrs. Durand and Geoffroy de Villeneuve, who have examined them like enlightened observers, and perfectly well described them in their travels, only that they have too much exaggerated the agricultural advantages of Cape Verd.

We shall not have the presumption to lay down plans, to propose systems, to enforce such or such means for putting them in execution. We shall merely terminate our task by some general considerations calculated to confirm what numerous and able observers have already thought, of the importance of the establishments in Africa, and of the necessity of adopting some general plan of colonisation for these countries.

However pride, prejudice and personal interest, may deceive themselves respecting the re-establishment of our Western Colonies, nobody will be able longer to dissemble the inutility of attempts to persevere in a false route. Calculation will at length triumph over blind obstinacy and false reasonings. There is already a certain number of incontestable data, the consequences of which must be one day admitted. And first, though some persons who fancy that, like them, the whole world have been asleep for these twenty-five or thirty years, still dream of the submission of St. Domingo, reasonable persons now acknowledge, that even were the final success of such an enterprise possible, its real result would be, to have expended, in order to conquer a desert, and ruins drenched in blood, ten times more men and money than would be sufficient to colonise Africa. It is well known, also, that the soil of Martinique is exhausted, and that its productions will diminish more and more; that the small extent of Guadaloupe confines its culture to a very narrow circle, and does not permit it to offer a mass of produce sufficient to add much to the force of the impulse, which a country like France, must give to all parts of its agricultural and commercial industry. It is not to be doubted, but that nature has given to French Guiyana the elements of great prosperity; but this establishment requires to be entirely created; every thing has hitherto concurred to prolong its infancy. There are not sufficient hands; and how will you convey thither the requisite number of cultivators, when you have proclaimed the abolition of the slave trade.

The Abolition of the Slave Trade: this is the principle, pregnant with consequences, which should induce every enlightened government speedily to change its whole colonial system. It would be in vain to attempt to prolong this odious trade by smuggling, and thus still to draw from it some precarious resources. This sad advantage would but keep open the wound which has struck the western colonies, without being able to effect their recovery, as is desired by those who seek to found their prosperity on the regular farming out of one of the races of mankind. The slave trade is abolished not only by religion, by treaties, by the consent of some powers, by the calculations and interest of some others, which will not permit it to be re-established; but it is abolished also by the light of the age, by the wish of all civilised nations; by opinion, that sovereign of the world, which triumphs over every obstacle, and subdues all that resist her laws. Without the slave trade, you cannot transport to the West Indies those throngs of men whose sweat and blood are the manure of your lands: on the other hand, you see the Genius of Independence hover over the New World, which will soon force you to seek friends and allies where you have hitherto reckoned only slaves. Why then do you hesitate to prepare a new order of things, to anticipate events, which time, whose march you cannot arrest, brings every day nearer and nearer? Reason, your own interest, the force of circumstances, the advantages of nature, the richness of the soil, every thing tells you that it is to Africa, that you must carry culture and civilization.

Without entering into the question, whether the Government should reserve to itself, exclusively, the right of founding colonies on that continent, or whether it ought to encourage colonial companies, and depend on the efforts of private interest suitably directed, let us be permitted to offer some views, on the prudent and temperate course which ought to be laid down, to arrive at a satisfactory result, not only in respect to the civilization of the blacks, but even relatively to the commercial advantages which the colonist must naturally have in view.

Though the abolition of the slave trade has been proclaimed, yet the present slaves must be led to liberty only in a progressive manner. The whites who are possessed of negroes, should not be allowed to prolong their possession and their dominion over them, beyond the space of ten years, and without being permitted to resell them during that period. During these ten years, the negroes should be prepared for their new condition as well by instruction as by the successive amelioration of their situation; it would be necessary gradually to relax the chain of slavery; and by affording them means to lay up a part of the produce of their labour, inspire them with the desire, and the necessity of possessing something of their own.

After these ten years, which may be called a Noviciate, it is to be presumed, that if lands were granted to them upon advantageous conditions, fixed before hand, if they were furnished in case of need, with the agricultural instruments, the use of which they would have learned, they would become excellent cultivators: it is needless to remark that the man who cultivates the soil, and whose labour the soil rewards, by its produce, becomes strongly attached to the land, which supplies both his wants and his enjoyments, and is soon led by family affections to the love of social order, and to the sentiments which constitute a good citizen.

The blacks have been too long encouraged to sell their fellow-creatures, for us to depend upon their soon forgetting this deplorable traffic. But doubtless we ought to begin by renouncing the perfidious means of inflaming their cupidity and their passions. The articles which they are the most desirous to obtain from us, ought to be the price of the produce of the soil, and no longer the means of exchange, and the aliment of this dreadful traffic in human flesh. It would, however, be proper that, as long as slaves should continue to arrive from the interior, the whites might buy them. This permission should be granted for a time, and in a certain extent of country. Their slavery should also be limited to ten years, as we have said above, and their moral and physical improvement, should be directed in such a manner as to attach them to the soil by exciting in them the love of property.

The laws and institutions which govern the mother country, would incontrovertibly be applicable to the new establishments. It would certainly be presumable, that on account of particular considerations of moral and political order, it would be proper to allow local regulations, in forming which, all proprietors enjoying the rights of citizenship, ought to participate, without any distinction of colour. It would especially be highly important, that the regulations for the government of the slaves, should be founded on mildness and humanity, that prudent and enlightened persons should superintend the execution of them, and have the necessary authority to prevent abuses, and to secure to the slave the protection of the law.

In order to obtain these results, it is evident that it would be no less essential to preserve the colonies from the scourge of arbitrary authority, from the excesses of power, which always accompany abuses, injustice, and corruption. When favor and caprice are the only laws that are attended to; when intrigue supplies the place of merit; when cupidity succeeds to honorable industry; when vice and meanness are titles to distinctions, and the true means of making a fortune; when honours are no longer synonimous with honour; then society presents only disorder and anarchy, then people renounce obscure virtue, and laborious acquisition to follow the easy ways of corruption; then enlightened men, for whom public esteem is a sterile recommendation, the true servants of the king, the faithful friends of their country, are forced to disappear, to withdraw from employments, and the interest of the public, as well as that of humanity, is miserably sacrificed to the basest calculations, to the most guilty passions.

He who desires the end, desires the means of attaining it. The end at present, should be to prepare every thing beforehand, and rather sooner than later, in order to repair in Africa the past losses and disasters, which irremediable events have caused in the Western Colonies, and to substitute for their riches their prosperity, the progressive decline of which is henceforward inevitable, new elements of wealth and prosperity: the means will be to carry into these countries, so long desolated by our relentless avarice, knowledge, cultivation, and industry. By these means we shall see in that vast continent numerous colonies arise, which will restore to the mother country all the splendour, all the advantages of her ancient commerce, and repay her with interest for the sacrifices she may have made in the new world. But to effect this, let there be no more secret enterprises; no more connivance at fraudulent traffic, no more unhappy negroes snatched away from their families; no more tears shed on that sad African soil, so long the witness of so many afflictions; no more human victims, dragged to the altars of the shameful, and insatiable divinities, which have already devoured such numbers: consequently, let there be no more grounds for hearing in the English Parliament, voices boldly impeaching our good faith, attacking the national honour, and possitively asserting that France maintains in her African possessions, the system of the slave trade in the same manner as she did before she consented to its abolition.

Africa offers to our speculators, to the enterprises of our industry, a virgin soil, and an inexhaustible population peculiarly fitted to render it productive. It must be our business to form them according to our views, by associating them in these by a common interest. In conquering them by benefits, instead of subjugating them by crimes, or degrading them by corruption, let us lead them to social order and to happiness, by our moral superiority, instead of dragging them under scourges and chains to misery and death, we shall then have accomplished a useful and a glorious enterprise; we shall have raised our commercial prosperity on the greatest interest of those who have been the voluntary instruments of it, and above all, we shall have expiated, by an immense benefit, this immense crime of the outrages, with which we so long afflicted humanity.

INTRODUCTION.

The following Notes were communicated to the Authors, when the second edition was already so far advanced, as to render it impracticable to incorporate them with the body of the work, and they are therefore placed at the end. Some of them are extracted from the Journal of Mr. Bredif, who belonged to the expedition, and were communicated by his uncle, Mr. Landry; the others are by an officer of merit, whose modesty prevents the publication of his name.

The Translator has thought it would be more convenient to place these notes in one series, refering to the pages to which they belong. Those of Mr. Bredif, are signed (B) the others (A).

NOTES.

I.—*Page 14.—On the Route to Africa.*

In going from Europe to the western coasts of Africa, situated to the north of the line, it is better still, to pass between the Azores and Madeira, and not to come within sight of the coast, till you have nearly reached the latitude of the point where you desire to land. Nothing but the necessity of procuring refreshments can authorise vessels, bound to the Cape of Good Hope, or to the south of America, to touch at the Canaries, or at the Cape Verd Islands. Notwithstanding the depth of the channels between the first of these islands, these seas, which are subject both to calms and hurricanes are not without danger. By keeping at a distance, there is also the advantage of avoiding the current of Gibraltar, and of not running the risk of meeting with the north west winds, which generally prevail along the desert, (and hitherto insufficiently known.) Coasts of Zaara, along which the Medusa sailed to no purpose, and which winds also tend to impel vessels upon the dangerous bank of Arguin. (A)

II.—*On the Manœuvres before Funchal.*

The usual indecision, which the commander of the frigate displayed in all his resolutions, joined to a little accident, made him change the intention which he had expressed of presenting himself before Funchal. From a singularity which nothing justified, he appeared to have more confidence in one of the passengers, who had indeed, frequented these seas, than in any of his officers, in respect to the management of the vessel. As they approached Madeira, the vessel was worked almost entirely according to the advice of this passenger; but suddenly the breeze, which is always strong in the neighbourhood of these mountainous countries, fell when they got too near it, the sails flagged, the current seemed rapid; but after some hesitation in the manœuvring of the vessel, which the officers soon put into proper order, they recovered the wind, and it was resolved to steer for Teneriffe. (A)

III.—*Page 22.—On the Islands of Madeira and Teneriffe.*

Madeira and Teneriffe seen on the side where their capital cities lie, have a very different appearance. The first is smiling with cultivation from its shores, almost to the summit of the mountains. Every where the eye discovers only little habitations surrounded by vineyards and orchards of the most delightful verdure: these modest dwellings surrounded by all the luxuriance of vegetation, placed under an azure sky, which is seldom obscured by clouds, seem to be the abode of happiness, and the navigator, long wearied by the monotonous prospect of the sea, cheerfully hailed this delightful prospect. Teneriffe, on the contrary, shews itself with every mark of the cause by which it was formed. The whole south east side is composed of black sterile rocks, which are piled together in an extraordinary confusion; even to the environs of the town of Saint Croix, scarcely any thing is seen, on the greater part of these dry and burnt lands, but low plants, the higher of which are probably Euphorbia, or thorny Cereus; and those which cover the ground, the hairy lichen, *Crocella tinctoria*, which is employed in dying, and which this island furnishes in abundance. Seen from the sea, the town, which is in the form of an amphitheatre, appears to be situated in the recess, formed by two distinct branches of mountains, of which the one towards the south, forms the Peak properly so called; it is particularly remarkable at a distance for its slender towers, and for the steeples of its churches, the construction of which, calls to mind the arabic architecture. (A)

IV.—*Page 22.—On the Mouth of the River St. John.*

There is probably an error in this account: the river St. John, is much more to the south, and on the north side of Cape Meric. The inlet, which was perceived during the ceremony of the tropic, which was a little tardy, is the gulf of St. Cyprian, into which the currents appear to set. Early in the morning, and to the north of this gulph, they passed a little island, very near the coast, and the black colour of which, owing doubtless to the marine plants that cover it, made a striking contrast with the whiteness of the sandy downs of the great desert, the abode of the Moors, and of wild beasts.—*Tellus leonum arida nutrix.* (A)

V.—*Page 24.—On the reconnaissance of Cape Blanco.*

Mr. de Chaumareys gave notice in the course of this day, that he had a mind to anchor at a cable's length from Cape Blanco. He talked of it till the evening, but on going to bed he thought no more about it; however, he continually repeated that the minister had ordered him to make that Cape; and therefore, when somebody said the next morning, that this Cape was supposed to have been seen at eight o'clock the preceding evening, it was from that time forbidden to doubt of it; and either from deference or persuasion it was agreed, but not without laughing, that the Cape had been seen at the hour mentioned. It was from the course of the vessel at this moment that the route was calculated till an observation was made at noon. (A)

VI.—*Page 25.—On the Refusal to answer the Signals of the Echo.*

It would probably have been of no use to inform Mr. de Chaumarey's of the signals of the Echo. The commander of the Medusa, the chief of the division, had declared already in the roads of the island of Aix, his intention to abandon his vessels, and to proceed alone in all haste to the Senegal. Though he spoke of strictly following the pretended instructions of the minister respecting the route to be followed, it was, however, violating the principle one, since it is useless to form a division if it is not to go together. The corvette, commanded by Mr. Venancourt succeeded, it is true, several times in joining the commander; but soon, by the superior sailing of the Medusa, they lost sight of him again, and every time they rejoiced at it. This resolution, not to sail in company, was the chief cause of the loss of the principal vessel. The Echo having determined, as was proper, to follow its commander, alone passed to the north west of the bank. The two other vessels which had remained long behind and were much more at liberty, passed more than thirty leagues to the west of it, and thus proved that it was the safest and shortest rout. (A)

VII.—*Page 31.—On the Stranding of the Medusa.*

From ten o'clock in the morning the colour of the water visibly changed, and the head pilot, calculating after his *sea-torch* before mentioned, declared, at half past eleven, that they were at the edge of the bank, and this was probable. From that moment the sailors were entirely employed in drawing up the lines thrown out alongside of the vessel, and the astonishing quantity of fish, all of the cod species, which were drawn on board, added to the weeds that floated on every side, were more than sufficient to make it believed that they were sailing upon a shoal. We shall speak below of the species of this fish; but as for the weeds, which were perceived on every side, besides that they gave reason to suppose that we were approaching the land, their appearance in this gulph, also gives ground to presume, that the currents of these seas, at this season, set north, since the plants, with exception of some *Zosterés*, were nothing but long stalks of grasses; most of them still furnished with their roots, and many even with their ears, belonging to the tall grasses of the banks of the Senegal, and the Gambia, which these rivers bring away at the time of the inundations. All those which could be observed were *Panios* or millets. (A)

VIII.—*Page 31.—Moment of the Stranding of the Frigate.*

The officers wanted to tack about, as the water became shallower every moment: but Mr. Richefort, (who enjoyed the confidence of Mr. de Chaumarey's,) declaring that there was no reason to be alarmed, the captain ordered more sail to be spread. Soon we had only fifteen fathoms, then nine, then six. By promptitude the danger might still have been avoided. They hesitated: two minutes afterwards a shock informed us that we had struck; the officers, at first astonished, gave their orders with a voice that shewed their agitation: the captain was wholly deprived of his; terror was painted on the countenances of all those who were capable of appreciating the danger: I thought it imminent, and expected to see the frigate bilge. I confess that I was not satisfied with myself, at this first moment, I could not help trembling, but afterwards, my courage did not any more forsake me. (B)

XI.—*Page 41.—Confusion on Board the Frigate.*

The frigate having stranded, the same thing happened, which usually does happen in critical circumstances, no decisive measures were taken: to increase our misfortunes the obedience of the crew to the officers was diminished for want of confidence. There was no concert. A great deal of time was spent, and the second day was lost without having done any thing.

On the third, preparations were made to quit the frigate, and the efforts made the day before to get her afloat, were renewed, but only half measures were taken. The other preparations to insure our safety were not carried on with any activity. Every thing went wrong. A list of the people was made, and they were distributed between the boats and the raft, in order that they might hold themselves ready to embark when it should be time. I was set down for the long boat.

Our mode of living, during all this time, was extremely singular. We all worked either at the pump or at the capstern. There was no fixed time for meals, we eat just as we could snatch an opportunity. The greatest confusion prevailed, the sailors already attempted to plunder the trunks. (B)

X.—*Page 43.—The Frigate lost.*

On the fourth the weather being fine, and the wind favourable to the motion which we wished to give to the vessel, we succeeded in it. The most ardent hope was excited among all the crew, we even supped very cheerfully; we flattered ourselves that we should free the vessel and sail the next day. A beautiful evening encouraged our hopes, we slept upon deck by moonlight; but at midnight the sky was overclouded, the wind rose, the sea swelled, the frigate began to be shaken. These shocks were much more dangerous than those in the night of the third. At three o'clock in the morningt he master-caulker came to tell the captain that the vessel had sprung a leak and was filling; we immediately flew to the pumps, but in vain, the hull was split, all endeavours to save the frigate were given up, and nothing thought of but how to save the people. (B)

XI.—*Page 53.—Embarkment of the Crew.*

On the 5th, about seven o'clock in the morning, all the soldiers were first embarked on board the raft, which was not quite finished, these unfortunate men crowded together upon pieces of wood, were in water up to the middle.

Mrs. and Miss Schmalz went on board their boat. Mr. Schmalz, notwithstanding the entreaties of every body, would not yet quit the vessel.

The people embarked in disorder, every body was in a hurry. I advised them to wait patiently till every one's turn came. I gave the example, and was near being the victim of it. All the boats, carried away by the current, withdrew and dragged the raft with them; there still remained sixty of us on board. Some sailors, thinking that the others were going to abandon them, loaded their muskets, and were going to fire upon the boats, and particularly upon the boat of the captain, who had already gone on board. It was with the greatest difficulty that I dissuaded them from it. I had need of all my strength, and all the arguments I could think of. I succeeded in seizing some loaded muskets and threw them into the sea.

When I was preparing to quit the frigate, I had contented myself with a small parcel of things which were indispensable; all the rest had been already pillaged. I had divided, with a comrade, eight hundred livres in gold, which I had still in my possession; this proved very fortunate for me in the sequel. This comrade had embarked on board one of the boats. (B)

XII.—*Page 54.—On Mr. Espiau.*

The name of this officer cannot be mentioned, in this memoir, without acknowledging the services which he performed on this occasion. To him we owe the lives of several sailors and soldiers who had remained on board It is he who, notwithstanding the various dangers with which he was surrounded, following only the impulse of his courage, succeeded in saving them. In giving him a command, the minister has paid the debt which the State had contracted towards this officer for his honorable conduct. (A)

XIII.—*Page 54.—Embarkation of the Men who remained on Board the Frigate.*

I began to believe that we were abandoned, and that the boats, being too full, could take no more people on board. The frigate was quite full of water. Being convinced that she touched the bottom, and that she could not sink, we did not lose courage. Without fearing death it was proper to do every thing we could to save ourselves: we joined all together, officers, sailors and soldiers. We appointed a master-pilot for our leader, we pledged our honour, either to save ourselves, or to perish all together; an officer and myself promised to remain to the last.

We thought of making another raft. We made the necessary preparations to cut away one of the masts, in order to ease the frigate. Exhausted by fatigue, it was necessary to think of taking some food; the gally was not under water; we lighted a fire; the pot was already boiling, when we thought we saw the long-boat returning to us; it was towed by two other lighter-boats, we all renewed the oath, either all to embark, or all to remain. It appeared to us that our weight would sink the long-boat.

Mr. Espiau, who commanded it, came on board the frigate, he said that he would take every body on board. First, two women and a child were let down; the most fearful followed. I embarked immediately before Mr. Espiau. Some men preferred remaining on board the frigate to sinking, as they said, with the long-boat. In fact, we were crowded in it to the number of ninety persons; we were obliged to throw into the sea our little parcels, the only things we had left. We did not dare to make the least motion for fear of upsetting our frail vessel.

I had had some water-casks and a great many bottles of wine put on board: I had got all these things ready before hand. The sailors concealed in the long-boat what ought to have been for every body; they drank the whole the first night, which exposed us to the danger of perishing with thirst in the sequel.(B)

XIV.—*Page 67.—Occurrences which took place after the Raft was abandoned.*

About half-past six in the evening, and just at sunset, the people in the boats descried the land: that is to say, the high downs of sand of the Zaara, which appeared quite brilliant and like heaps of gold and silver. The sea, between the frigate and the coast, appeared to have some depth; the waves were longer and more hollow, as if the bank of Arguin rose towards the West. But as they approached the land, the water suddenly became shallow, and finding only a depth of three or four feet, they resolved to cast anchor till day-break. Several scattered hills, a few rocky shoals nearly dry, made them presume that they were in the Lagunes, formed by the River St. John; this opinion was verified by the sight of Cape Meric, which appears like the continuation of a high hill coming from the interior, but suddenly rising at its approach to the sea, like the torrents of Volcanic matter. In passing before this cape, out at sea and towards the West, the sea appeared to break over some shoals, which are suspected to be the Southern end of the bank of Arguin, which, according to some persons at Senegal, is dry at low water. (A)

XV.—*Page 68.—Forsaking the Raft.*

When we had overtaken the raft, towed by the other boats, we asked the latter to take from us at least twenty men, or otherwise we should sink. They answered that they were already too much loaded. One of our movements, towards the boats, made them fancy that despair had inspired us with the idea of sinking them and ourselves at the same time.

How could the officers imagine that such a design was entertained by Mr. Espiau, who had just before displayed such a noble desire to assist his comrades? The boats, in order to avoid us, cut the ropes which united them together, and made all the sail they could from us. In the midst of this confusion, the rope which towed the raft, broke also, and a hundred and fifty men were abandoned in the midst of the ocean, without any hope of relief.

This moment was horrible. Mr. Espiau, to induce his comrades to make a last effort, tacked and made a motion to rejoin the raft. The sailors endeavoured to oppose it, saying that the men on the raft would fall upon us, and cause us all to perish. "I know it, my friends," said he, " but I will not approach so near as to incur any " danger; if the other vessels do not follow me, I will " think only on your preservation, I cannot do impossibili- " ties." In fact, seeing that he was not seconded, he resumed his route. The other boats were already far off. "We shall sink," cried Mr. Espiau, let us shew courage to the very last. Let us do what we can : *vive le roi!* This cry a thousand times repeated rises from the bosom of the waters which are to serve us for a grave. The boats also repeated it, we were near enough to hear this cry of *vive le roi!* Some of us thought that this enthusiasm was madness: was it the fulness of despair which made them speak so, or was it the expression of the soul broken by misfortune? I know not, but for my part, this moment appeared to me sublime: this cry was a rallying cry, a cry of encouragement and resignation. (B)

XVI.—*Page 84, line 3.—On the sudden Gale experienced by the Raft.*

This strong gale was the same North West wind which in this season, as has been said before, blows every day with great violence after sun-set; but which, that day, began sooner, and continued till 4 o'clock the next morning, when it was succeeded by a calm. The two boats which resisted it, were several times on the point of being wrecked. The whole time that this gale lasted, the sea was covered with a remarkable quantity of *galères* or *physalides,* (physalis pelasgica) which arranged, for the most part, in straight lines, and in two or three files, cut at an angle the direction of the waves, and seemed at the same time to present their crest or sail to the wind, in an oblique manner, as if to be less exposed to its impulse. It is probable that these animals have the faculty of sailing two or three abreast, and of ranging themselves in a regular or symetrical order; but had the wind surprised these, so arranged on the surface of the sea, and before they had time to sink, and shelter themselves at the bottom, or did the sea, agitated on these shores, to a greater depth than is supposed, make them fear, in this situation, to be thrown upon the coast? However it be, the orders of their march; their disposition, in respect to the force which impelled them, and which they strove to resist; the apparent stiffness of the sail seemed equally admirable and surprising. Mr. Rang, who has been mentioned with praise in this work, having had the curiosity to catch one of these singular animals, soon felt a tingling in his hand, and a burning heat, which made him feel much pain till the next day. Bones of *sèche gigantesque* (sepia, cuttle-fish) already whitened by the sun, passed rapidly along the side of the ship, and almost always with some insects, which having, imprudently ventured too far from the land, had taken refuge on these floating islands. As soon as the sea grew calm, they perceived some large pelicans, gently rocking themselves on the bosom of the waves. (A)

XVII.—*Page 151.—Landing of the Sixty-three Men of the Long-Boat.*

The sea was within two fingers breadth of the gunnale of the boat: the slighest wave entered; besides, it had a leak; it was necessary to empty it continually: a service which the soldiers and sailors, who were with me, refused. Happily the sea was pretty calm.

On the same evening, the 5th, we saw the land, and the cry of " land, land," was repeated by every body. We were sailing rapidly towards the coast of Africa, when we felt that we had struck upon the bottom. We were again in distress: we had but three feet water; but would it be possible for us to get the boat afloat again, and put out into the open sea? There was no more hope of being able to reach the shore. As for myself, I saw nothing but danger on the coast of Africa, and I preferred drowning to being made a slave, and conducted to Morocco or Algiers. But the long-boat grounded only once; we proceeded on our route, and by frequent soundings we got into the open sea towards night.

Providence had decided that we should experience fears of every kind, and that we should not perish What a night indeed was this! The sea ran very high, the ability of our pilot saved us. A single false manœuvre, and we must all have perished. We, however, partly shipped two or three waves which we were obliged to empty immediately. Any other boat, in the same circumstances, would have been lost. This long and dreadful night was at length succeeded by day.

At day break we found ourselves in sight of land. The sea became a little calm. Hope revived in the souls of the desponding sailors, almost every body desired to go on shore. The officer, in spite of himself, yielded to their wishes. We approached the coast and threw out a little anchor that we might not run aground. We were so happy as to come near the shore, where there was only two feet water. Sixty-three men threw themselves into the water and reached the shore, which is only a dry and burning sand, it must have been a few leagues above Portendic. I took care not to imitate them. I remained with about twenty-six others in the long-boat, all determined to endeavour to reach the Senegal with our vessel, which was lightened of above two-thirds of its burden. It was the 6th of July. (B)

XVIII.—*Page 152.—The Fifteen Persons in the Yawl taken into the Long-Boat ; sequel of the day of the 6th.*

An hour after landing the sixty-three men, we perceived behind us four of our boats. Mr. Espiau, notwithstanding the cries of his crew who opposed it, lowered his sails and lay-to, in order to wait for them. " They have " refused to take any people from us, let us do better now

" we are lightened, let us offer to take some from them." In fact, he made them this offer when they were within hail; but instead of approaching boldly, they kept at a distance. The smallest of the boats (a yawl) went from one to the other to consult them. This distrust came from their thinking, that, by a stratagem, we had concealed all our people under the benches, to rush upon them when they should be near enough, and so great was this distrust that they resolved to fly us like enemies. They feared every thing from our crew, whom they thought to be in a state of mutiny: however, we proposed no other condition on receiving some people, than to take in some water, of which we began to be in want, as for biscuit we had a sufficient stock.

Above an hour had passed after this accident, when the sea ran very high. The yawl could not hold out against it: being obliged to ask assistance, it came up to us. My comrade de Chasteluz was one of the fifteen men on board of her. We thought first of his safety, he leaped into our boat, I caught him by the arm to hinder his falling into the sea, we pressed each others hands, what language.

Singular concatenation of events! If our sixty-three men had not absolutely insisted upon landing, we could not have saved the fifteen men in the yawl; we should have had the grief of seeing them perish before our eyes, without being able to afford them any assistance: this is not all, the following is what relates to myself personally. A few minutes before we took in the people of the yawl, I had undressed myself in order to dry my clothes, which had been wet for forty-eight hours, from my having assisted in lading the water out of the long-boat. Before I took off my pantaloons I felt my purse, which contained the four hundred francs; a moment after I had lost it; this was the completion of all my misfortunes. What a happy thought was it to have divided my eight hundred francs with Mr. de Chasteluz who now had the other four hundred.

The heat was very violent on the sixth. We were reduced to an allowance of one glass of dirty or corrupted water; and therefore to check our thirst, we put a piece of lead into our mouths; a melancholy expedient!

The night returned; it was the most terrible of all: the light of the moon shewed us a raging sea: long and hollow waves threatened twenty times to swallow us up. The pilot did not believe it possible to avoid all those which came upon us; if we had shipped a single one it would have been all over with us. The pilot must have let the helm go, and the boat would have sunk. Was it not in fact better to disappear at once than to die slowly?

Towards the morning the moon having set, exhausted by distress, fatigue, and want of sleep I could not hold out any longer and fell asleep; notwithstanding the waves which were ready to swallow me up. The Alps and their picturesque scenery rose before my imagination. I enjoyed the freshness of their shades, I renewed the delicious moments which I have passed there, and as if to enhance my present happiness by the idea of past evils, the remembrance of my good sister flying with me into the woods of Kaiserslautern to escape the Cossacks, is present to my fancy. My head hung over the sea; the noise of the waves dashing against our frail bark, produced on my senses the effect of a torrent falling from the summit of a mountain. I thought I was going to plunge into it. This pleasing illusion was not complete; I awoke, and in what a state! I raised my head with pain; I open my ulcerated lips, and my parched tongue finds on them only a bitter crust of salt, instead of a little of that water which I had seen in my dream. The moment was dreadful, and my despair was extreme. I thought of throwing myself into the sea, to terminate at once all my sufferings. This despair was of short duration, there was more courage in suffering.

A hollow noise, which we heard in the distance, increased the horrors of this night. Our fears, that it might be the bar of the Senegal, hindered us from making so much way as we might have done. This was a great error; the noise proceeded from the breakers which are met with on all the coasts of Africa. We found afterwards, that we were above sixty leagues from the Senegal. (B)

XIX.—*Page* 162.—*Stranding of the Long-Boat, and Two other Boats.*

Our situation did not change till the eighth; we suffered more and more from thirst. The officer desired me to make a list, and to call the people to distribute the allowance of water; every one came and drank what was given him. I held my list under the tin cup, to catch the drops which fell, and moisten my lips with them. Some persons attempted to drink sea water; I am of opinion that they did but hasten the moment of their destruction.

About the middle of the day, on the 8th of July, one of our boats sailed in company with the long-boat. The people on board suffered more than we, and resolved to go on shore and get water if possible; but the sailors mutinied and insisted on being landed at once: they had drank nothing for two days. The officers wished to oppose it; the sailors were armed with their sabres. A dreadful butchery was on the point of taking place on board this unfortunate boat. The two sails were hoisted in order to strand more speedily upon the coast, every body reached the shore, the boat filled with water and was abandoned.

This example, fatal to us, gave our sailors an inclination to do the same. Mr. Espian consented to land them; he hoped to be able afterwards with the little water that remained, and by working the vessel ourselves, to reach the Senegal. We therefore placed ourselves round this little water, and took our swords to defend it. We advanced near to the breakers, the anchor was got up, and the officer gave orders to let the boat's painter go gently, the sailors on the contrary, either let the rope go at once, or cut it. Our boat being no longer checked, was carried into the first breaker. The water passed over our heads, and three quarters filled the boat: it did not sink. Immediately we hoisted a sail which carried us through the other breakers. The boat entirely filled and sunk, but there was only four feet water; every body leaped into the sea, and no one perished.

Before we thought of landing I had undressed myself, in order to dry my clothes; I might have put them on again, but the resolution to land having been taken, I thought that without clothes, I should be more able to swim in case of need. Mr. de Chasteluz could not swim: he fastened a rope round his middle, of which I took one end, and by means of which, I was to draw him to me as soon as I got on shore. When the boat sunk I threw myself into the water, I was very glad that I touched the bottom, for I was uneasy about my comrade. I returned to the boat to look for my clothes and my sword. A part of them had been already stolen, I found only my coat and one of the two pair of pantaloons which I had with me. A negro offered to sell me an old pair of shoes for eight francs, for I wanted a pair of shoes to walk in.

The sailors had saved the barrel of water; and as soon

as we were on shore they fought for the drinking of it. I rushed in among them, and made my way to him who had got the barrel at his mouth. I snatched it from him and contrived to swallow two mouthfuls, the barrel was afterwards taken from me, but these two mouthfuls did me as much good as two bottles; but for them I could not have lived longer than a few hours.

Thus I found myself on the coast of Africa wet to the skin, with nothing in my pockets except a few biscuits, steeped in salt water, to support me for several days: without water, amidst a sandy desert inhabited by a ferocious race of men: thus we had left one danger to plunge into a greater.

We resolved to proceed along the sea coast, because the breeze cooled us a little, and besides the moist sand was softer than the fine moveable sand in the interior. Before we proceeded on our march, we waited for the crew of the other boat which had stranded before us.

We had proceeded about half an hour, when we perceived another boat advancing with full sail, and came with such violence on the beach that it stranded: it contained all the family of Mr. Picard, consisting of himself and his wife, three daughters grown up, and four young children, one of whom was at the breast. I threw myself into the sea to assist this unhappy family; I contributed to get Mr. Picard on shore, every body was saved. I went to look for my clothes, but could not find them; I fell into a violent passion, and expressed in strong terms, the infamy of stealing in such circumstances. I was reduced to my shirt and my trowsers. I know not whether my cries, and my complaints, excited remorse in the robber, but I found my coat and pantaloons again, a little further off upon the sand. (B)

XX.—*Page* 162.—*March in the Desert and Arrival at St. Louis.*

We proceeded on our journey for the rest of the day on the 8th of July; many of us were overcome by thirst. Many with haggard eyes awaited only death. We dug in the sand, but found only water more salt than that of the sea.

At last we resolved to pass the sandy downs along the sea coast; we afterwards met with a sandy plain almost as low as the ocean. On this sand there was a little long and hard grass. We dug a hole three or four feet deep, and found water which was whitish and had a bad smell. I tasted it and finding it sweet, cried out " we are saved!" These words were repeated by the whole caravan who collected round this water, which every one dveoured with his eyes. Five or six holes were soon made and every one took his fill of this muddy beverage. We remained two hours at this place, and endeavoured to eat a little biscuit in order to keep up our strength.

Towards evening we returned to the sea shore. The coolness of the night permitted us to walk, but Mr. Picard's family could not follow us. The children were carried, the officers setting the example, in order to induce the sailors to carry them by turns. The situation of Mr. Picard was cruel; his young ladies and his wife displayed great courage; they dressed themselves in mens clothes. After an hours march Mr. Picard desired that we might stop, he spoke in the tone of a man who would not be refused; we consented, though the least delay might endanger the safety of all. We stretched ourselves upon the sand, and slept till three o'clock in the morning.

We immediately resumed our march. It was the 9th

of July. We still proceeded along the sea shore, the wet sand was more easy to walk upon; we rested every half hour on account of the ladies.

About eight o'clock in the morning we went a little from the coast to reconnoitre some Moors who had shewn themselves. We found two or three wretched tents, in which there were some Mooresses almost all naked, they were as ugly and frightful as the sands they inhabit. They came to our aid, offering us water, goat's milk, and millet, which are their only food. They would have appeared to us handsome, if it had been for the pleasure of obliging us, but these rapacious creatures wanted us to give them every thing we had. The sailors, who were loaded with what they had pillaged from us, were more fortunate than we, a handkerchief procured them a glass of water or milk, or a handful of millet. They had more money than we, and gave pieces of five or ten francs for things, for which we offered twenty sous. These Mooresses, however, did not know the value of money, and delivered more to a person who gave them two or three little pieces of ten sous, than to him who offered them a crown of six livres Unhappily we had no small money, and I drank more than one glass of milk at the rate of six livres per glass.

We bought, at a dearer price than we could have bought gold, two goats which we boiled by turns in a little metal kettle belonging to the Mooresses. We took out the pieces half boiled, and devoured them like savages. The sailors, for whom we had bought these goats, scarcely left the officers their share, but seized what they could, and still complained of having had too little. I could not help speaking to them as they deserved. They consequently had a spite against me and threatened me more than once.

At four o'clock in the afternoon, after we had passed the greatest heat of the day in the disgusting tents of the Mooresses, stretched by their side, we heard a cry of "*To arms, to arms!*" I had none; I took a large knife which I had preserved, and which was as good as a sword. We advanced towards some Moors and Negroes, who had already disarmed several of our people whom they had found reposing on the sea shore. The two parties were on the point of coming to blows, when we understood that these men came to offer to conduct us to Senegal.

Some timid persons distrusted their intentions. For myself, as well as the most prudent among us, I thought that we should trust entirely to men who came in a small number, and who, in fact, confided their own safety to us; though it would have been so easy for them, to come insufficiently large numbers to overwhelm us. We did so, and experience proved that we did well.

We set off with our Moors who were very well made and fine men of their race; a Negro, their slave was one of the handsomest men I have ever seen. His body of a fine black, was clothed in a blue dress which he had received as a present. This dress became him admirably, his gait was proud and his air inspired confidence. The distrust of some of our Negroes, who had their arms unsheathed, and fear painted on the countenances of some made him laugh. He put himself in the middle of them, and placing the point of the weapons upon his breast, opened his arms, to make them comprehend that he was not afraid, and that they also ought not to fear him.

After we had proceeded some time, night being come, our guides conducted us a little inland, behind the downs where there were some tents inhabited by a pretty considerable number of Moors. Many persons in our caravan cried out, that they were going to be led to death. But we did not listen to them, persuaded that in every way we were undone, if the Moors were resolved on our destruction, that besides, it was their true interest to conduct us to Senegal, and that in short, confidence was the only means of safety.

Fear caused every body to follow us. We found in the camp, water, camels' milk, and dry, or rather rotten fish. Though all these things were enormously dear, we were happy to meet with them. I bought for ten francs one of these fish which stunk terribly. I wrapt it up in the only handkerchief I had left, to carry it with me. We were not sure of always finding such a good inn upon the road. We slept in our usual bed, that is to say stretched upon the sand. We had rested till midnight: we took some asses for Mr. Picard's family, and for some men whom fatigue had rendered incapable of going any further.

I observed that the men who were most overcome by fatigne were presisely those who were the most robust. From their look and their apparent strength they might have been judged indefatigable, but they wanted mental strength, and this alone supports man in such a crisis. For my part I was astonished at bearing so well so many fatigues and privations. I suffered, but with courage; my stomach, to my great satisfaction did not suffer at all. I bore every thing in the same manner till the last.

Sleep alone, but the most distressing sleep possible, had nearly caused my destruction. It was at two or three o'clock in the morning that it seized me, I slept as I walked. As soon as they cried halt I let myself fall upon the sand and was plunged into the most profound lethergy. Nothing gave me more pain than to hear at the expiration of a quarter of an hour " *up, march.*"

I was once so overcome that I heard nothing, I remained stretched upon the ground while the whole caravan passed by me. It was already at a great distance when a straggler happily perceived me; he pushed me, and at last succeeded in awaking me. But for him I should doubtless have slept several hours. If I had awoke alone in the middle of the desert, either despair would have terminated my sufferings, or I should have been made a slave by the Moors, which I could not have borne. To avoid this misfortune I begged one of my friends to watch over me, and to waken me at every stage, which he did.

On the 10th of July towards six o'clock in the morning, we were marching along the sea coast, when our guide gave us notice to be upon our guard and to take our arms. I seized my knife; the whole party was collected. The country was inhabited by a poor and plundering race of Moors, who would not have failed to attack those who had loitered behind. The precaution was good, some Moors shewed themselves on the downs; their number encreased and soon exceeded ours. To move them, we placed ourselves in a line holding our swords and sabres in the air. Those who had no arms waved the scabbards, to make them believe that we were all armed with muskets. They did not approach. Our guides went half way to meet them. They left one man and retired: the Moors did the same on their side. The two deputies conversed together for some time, then each returned to his party. The explanation was satisfactory, and the Moors soon came to us without the leasr distrust.

Their women brought us milk which they sold horribly dear; the rapacity of these Moors is astonishing, they insisted on having a share of the milk, which they had sold us.

Mean time we saw a sail advancing towards us: we made all kinds of signals to be perceived by it, and we were convinced that they were answered. Our joy was lively and well founded: it was the Argus brig which came to our assistance, She lowered her sails and hoisted out a boat. When it was near the breakers a Moor threw himself into the sea, carrying a note which painted our distress. The boat took the Moor on board and returned with the note to the captain. Half an hour afterwards the boat returned laden with a large barrel, and two small ones. When it reached the place where it had taken in the Moor, the latter threw himself into the sea again to bring back the answer. It informed us that they were going to throw into the sea a barrel of biscuit and cheese, and two others containing brandy and wine.

Another piece of news filled us with joy; the two boats which had not stranded on the coast as we had done arrived at the Senegal, after having experienced the most stormy weather. Without losing a moment the governor had dispatched the Argus, and taken every measure to assist the shipwrecked people, and to go to the Medusa. Besides, he had sent by land camels loaden with provisions to meet us, lastly, the Moors were desired to respect us, and to render us assistance: so much good news revived us, and gave us fresh courage.

I learned also that Mr. Schmalz and his family, those very ladies, whom I had seen expose themselves with so much composure to the fury of the waves, and who had made me shed the only tears which our misfortunes had drawn from me, were well and in safety. I should have been sorry to die without having learned that they were preserved.

When the three barrels were thrown into the sea we

followed them with our eyes; we feared lest the current, instead of bringing them to the coast, should carry them into the open sea. At last we saw, clearly, that they approached us. Our Negroes and Moors swam to them, and pushed them to the coast, where we secured them.

The great barrel was opened: the biscuit and cheese were distributed. We would not open those of wine and brandy. We feared lest the Moors, at this sight, would not be able to refrain from falling upon the booty. We continued our march, and about half a league farther on, made a delicious feast on the sea-shore. Our strength being revived, we continued our route with more ardour.

Towards the close of the day, the aspect of the country began to change a little. The downs were lower: we perceived, at a distance, a sheet of water: we thought, and this was no small satisfaction to us, that it was the Senegal which made an elbow in this place to run parallel to the sea. From this elbow runs the little rivulet called *Marigot des Maringoins;* we left the sea-shore to pass it a little higher up. We reached a spot where there was some verdure and water, and resolved to remain there till midnight.

We had scarcely reached this spot, when we saw an Englishman coming towards us with three or four Marabous, or priests; they had camels with them; they were doubtless sent by the English Governor of Senegal, to seek for the shipwrecked people. One of the camels, laden with provisions, is immediately dispatched; those who conduct it are to go, if necessary, to Portendic, to fetch our companions in misfortune; or at least to get some information respecting them.

The English envoy had money to buy us provisions. He informed us that we had still three days march to the

Senegal. We imagined that we were nearer to it; the most fatigued were terrified at this great distance. We slept all together on the sand. Nobody was suffered to go to a distance for fear of the lions, which were said to haunt this country. This fear did not at all alarm me, nor hinder me from sleeping pretty well.

On the 11th of July, after having walked from one o'clock in the morning till seven, we arrived at a place where the Englishman expected to meet with an ox. By some misunderstanding there was none; we were obliged *to pinch our bellies:* but we had a little water.

The heat was insupportable; the sun was already scorching. We halted on the white sand of these downs, as being more wholesome for a resting place than the sand wetted by the sea-water. But this sand was so hot, that even the hands could not endure it. Towards noon we were broiled by the beams of the sun darting perpendicularly upon our heads. I found no remedy, except in a creeping plant, which grew here and there on the moving sand. I set up some old stalks, and spread over them my coat and some leaves: thus I put my head in the shade; the rest of my body was roasted. The wind overturned, twenty times, my slight scaffolding.

Meantime, the Englishman was gone, on his camel, to see after an ox. He did not return till four or five o'clock: when he informed us that we should find this animal, after we had proceeded some hours. After a most painful march, till night, we, in fact, met with an ox which was small, but tolerably fat. We looked at some distance from the sea, for a place where there was supposed to be a spring. It was only a hole, which the Moors had left a few hours before. Here we fixed ourselves, a dozen fires were lighted around us. A negro twisted the neck of the ox, as we should have done that of a fowl. In five minutes it was flayed and cut into pieces, which we toasted on the points of our swords or sabres. Every one devoured his portion.

After this slight repast, we all lay down to sleep. I was not able to sleep: the tiresome buzzing of the mosquitoes, and their cruel stings, prevented me, though I was so much in need of repose.

On the 12th, we resumed our march at three o'clock in the morning. I was indisposed; and to knock me up entirely, we had to walk over the moving sand of the point of Barbary. Nothing hitherto, had been more fatiguing: every body complained; our Moorish guides assured us that this way was shorter by two leagues. We preferred returning to the beach, and walking on the sand, which the sea-water rendered firm. This last effort was almost beyond my strength, I sunk under it, and but for my comrades, I should have remained upon the sand.

We had absolutely resolved to reach the point, where the river joins the downs. There some boats, which were coming up the river, were to take us on board, and convey us to St. Louis. When we had nearly reached this spot, we crossed the downs, and enjoyed the sight of the river which we had so long desired to meet with.

Happily too, it was the season when the water of the Senegal is fresh: we quenched our thirst at our pleasure. We stopped at last; it was only eight o'clock in the morning. We had no shelter during the whole day, except some trees, which were of a kind unknown to me, and which had a sombre foliage. I frequently went into the river, but without venturing too far from the bank, for fear of the alligators.

About two o'clock, a small boat arrived; the master

of it asked for Mr. Picard; he was sent by one of the old friends of that gentleman, and brought him provisions and clothes for his family. He gave notice to us all, in the name of the English Governor, that two other boats loaded with provisions, were coming. Having to wait till they arrived, I could not remain with Mr. Picard's family. I know not what emotion arose in my soul when I saw the fine white bread cut, and the wine poured out, which would have given me so much pleasure. At four o'clock we also were able to eat bread and good biscuit, and to drink excellent Madeira, which was lavished on us with little prudence. Our sailors were drunk; even those among us who had been more cautious, and whose heads were stronger, were, to say the least, very merry. How did our tongues run as we went down the river in our boats! After a short and happy navigation, we landed at Saint Louis, about seven o'clock in the evening.

But what should we do? whither should we go? Such were our reflections when we set foot on shore. They were not of long duration. We met with some of our comrades belonging to the boats who had arrived before us, who conducted us, and distributed us among various private houses, where every thing had been prepared to receive us well. I shall always remember the kind hospitality which was shewn to us, in general, by the white inhabitants of St. Louis, both English and French. We were all made welcome; we had all clean linen to put on, water to wash our feet; a sumptuous table was ready for us. As for myself, I was received, with several of my companions, in the house of Messrs. Potin and Durecur, Merchants of Bordeaux. Every thing they possessed was lavished upon us. They gave me linen, light clothes, in short, whatever I wanted. I had nothing left. Honour to him, who knows so well how to succour the unfortunate; to him especially who does it with so much simplicity, and as little ostentation as these gentlemen did. It seemed that it was a duty for them to assist every body. They would willingly have left to others no share in the good that was to be done. English officers eagerly claimed the pleasure, as they expressed it, of having some of the shipwrecked people to take care of. Some of us had feather beds, others good mattrasses laid upon mats, which they found very comfortable. I slept ill notwithstanding, I was too much fatigued, too much agitated: I always fancied, myself either bandied about by the waves, or treading on the burning sands. (B)

XXI.—*Page 178.—On the Manufactures of the Moors.*

The Moors tan skins with the dried pods of the Gummiferous Accia: thus prepared, they are impenetrable to the rain, and it may be affirmed that, for their suppleness, as well as for the brilliancy and finesss of their grain, they might become a valuable fur in Europe, either for use or ornament. The most beautiful of these skins seemed to be those of very young goats, taken from the belly of the dam before the time of gestation is completed. The great numbers of these animals, which are found round all the inhabited places, allow the inhabitants to sacrifice many to this species of luxury, without any extraordiny loss. The cloaks, with a hood, which are mentioned in this memoir, are composed of several of these skins, ingeniously sewed together, with small and very fine seams. These garments, designed as a protection against the cold and the rain, are generally black, but some are also seen of a reddish colour, which are not so beautiful, and heavier these latter are made of the skins of the kind of sheep, known by the name of guinea-sheep, which have hair instead of wool. As for the goldsmiths work, made by these people, it is executed by travelling workmen, who are at the same time armourers, smiths and jewellers. Furnished with a leather bag which is provided with an iron pipe, and filled with air, which they press and fill alternately, by putting it under their thigh, which they keep in constant motion, singing all the while; seated before a little hole dug in the sand, and under the shade of some leaves of the date-tree laid upon their heads, they execute on a little anvil, and with the help of a hammer, and some small iron awls, not only all kinds of repairs necessary to fire-arms, sabres, &c. but manufacture knives and daggers, and also make bracelets, earrings, and necklaces of gold, which they have the art of drawing into very fine wire, and forming into ornaments for women, in a manner which, though it wants taste, makes us admire the skill of the workman, especially when we consider the nature, and the small number of the tools which he employs.

The Moors, like the Mahometan negroes, are for the most part, provided with a larger or smaller number of *gris-gris*, a kind of talisman consisting in words, or verses copied from the Coran, to which they ascribe the power of securing them against diseases, witchcraft and accidents, and which they buy of their priests or Marabous. Some Spaniards from Teneriffe, who came to Cape Verd, at the time that the French Expedition had taken refuge there, struck us all, by their resemblance with these Africans. It was not only by their brown complexions that they resembled them; but it was also by their long rosaries, twisted in the same manner about their arms, resembling, except the cross, those of the Moors, and by the great number of Amulets, (*gris-gris* of another kind) which they wear round their necks, and by which they seemed to wish to rival the infidels in credulity. There is then, in the South of Europe, as well as in the North of Africa, a class of men, who would found their authority, upon ignorance, and derive their authority from superstition.

XXII.—*Page 235.—On the Bark given to the Sick.*

The bark, which began to be administered at that time, had been damaged, but an attempt was made to supply the want of it by the bark which the negroes use to cure the dysentery, and which they bring from the environs of Rufisque. This bark, of which they made a secret, seems to come from some terebinthine plant, and perhaps, from the *monbins*, which are common on this part of the coast. In the winter fevers which prevail at Goree, Cape Verd, &c. two methods of cure were employed which had different effects. These fevers were often attended with cholic, spasms in the stomach, and diarrhea. The first method consisted in vomitting, purging, and then administering the bark, to which musk was sometimes added, when the disorder grew worse. In this case, when the disease did not end in death, the fever was often succeeded by dysentery, or those who believed themselves cured, were subject to relapses. The second method, which Doctor Bergeron employed with more success, was opposite to the former; he vomited the patients but little, or not at all, endeavouring to calm the symptoms, to strengthen the patient by bitters, and at the last, he administered the bark.*

---

* It is to be observed that the author, in these two passages, uses the word *Kina* or Peruvian bark.--T.

The Negroes who, like all other people, have a materia medica, and pharmacopeia of their own, and who at this season, are subject to the same disorders as the Europeans, have recourse at the very beginning, to a more heroic remedy, and such of our soldiers encamped at Daccard, as made use of it, in general found benefit from it. The Priest or Marabous, who often offered them the assistance of his art, made them take a large glass of rum-punch, very warm, with a slight infusion of cayenne pepper. An extraordinary perspiration generally terminated this fit. The patient then avoided, for some days, walking in the sun, and eat a small quantity of roasted fish and cous-cous, mixed with a sufficient quantity of cassia leaves of different species, to operate as a gentle purgative. In order to keep up the perspiration, or according to the Negro Doctor, to strengthen the skin, he applied from time to time, warm lotions of the leaves of the palma christi, and of cassia. *(casse puante.)* The use of rum, which is condemned by the Mahometan religion, and is a production foreign to this country, gives reason to suppose that the remedy is of modern date, among the Negroes.

XXIII.—*Page* 283.—*On the Isle of St. Louis.*

St. Louis is a bank of scorching sand, without drinkable water or verdure, with a few tolerable houses towards the South, and a great number of low smoky straw huts, which, occupy almost all the North part. The houses are of brick, made of a salt clay, *(argile salée)* which the wind reduces to powder, unless they are carefully covered with a layer of chalk or lime, which it is difficult to procure, and the dazzling whiteness of which injures the eyes.

Towards the middle of this town, if it may be so

called, is a large manufactory in ruins, which is honored with the name of a fort, and of which the English have sacrificed a part, in order to make apartments for the governor, and to make the ground floor more airy, to quarter troops in it.

Opposite is a battery of heavy cannon, the parapet of which covers the square, on which are some trees, planted in strait lines for ornament. These trees are oleaginous Benjamins *(Bens Olefères)* which give no shade, and ought to be replaced by tamarinds, or sycamores, which are common in this neighbourhood, and would thrive well on this spot. None but people uncertain of their privilege to trade on this river, merchants who came merely to make a short stay, and indolent speculators would have contented themselves with this bank of burning sand, and not have been tempted by the cool shades and more fertile lands, which are within a hundred toises, but which, indeed, labour alone could render productive. Every thing is wretched in this situation.

Saint Louis is but a halting place in the middle of the river, where merchants who were going up it to seek slaves and gum, moored their vessels, and deposited their provisions, and the goods they had brought with them to barter.

What is said in the narrative of the means of attacking this port, is correct. When the enemy have appeared, the Negroes have always been those who have defended it with the most effect. But unhappily, there, as in the Antilles, persons are already to be found, who are inclined to hold out their hands to the English.

At Louis there are some palm-trees, and the lantara flabelliformis. Some little gardens have been made; but a cabbage, or a salad, are still of some value. Want, the mother of industry, obliged some of the inhabitants, during the war, to turn their thoughts to cultivation, and it should be the object of the government to encourage them.

XXIV.—*Page 303.—On the Islands of Goree and Cape Verd.*

At the distance of 1200 toises from the Peninsula of Cape Verd, a large black rock rises abruptly, from the surface of the sea. It is cut perpendicularly on one side, inaccessible in two-thirds of its circumference, and terminates, towards the south, in a low beach which it commands, and which is edged with large stones, against which the sea dashes violently. This beach, which is the prolongation of the base of the rock, bends in an arch, and forms a recess, where people land as they can. At the extremity of this beach is a battery of two or three guns; on the beach of the landing-place, is an epaulement, with embrasures which commands it. The town stands on this sand bank, and a little fort, built on the ridge of the rock, commands and defends it. In its present state, Goree could not resist a ship of the line. Its road, which is only an anchoring place in the open sea, is safe in the most stormy weather; but it is exposed to all winds except those that blow from the island, which then serves to shelter it.

The Europeans who desire to carry on the slave trade, have preferred this arid rock, placed in the middle of a raging rea, to the neighbouring continent, where they would find water, wood, vegetables, and in short, the necessaries of life. The same reason which has caused the preference to be given to a narrow and barren sand bank, in the middle of the Senegal to build St. Louis, has also decided in favor of Goree: it is, that both of them are but dens, or prisons, intended as a temporary confinement for wretches who, in any other situation, would find means to escape. To deal in men, nothing is wanting but fetters and jails, but as this kind of gain no longer exists, if it is wished to derive other productions from these possessions, and not to lose them entirely, it will be necessary to change the nature of our speculations, and to direct our views and our efforts to the continent, where industry and agriculture promise riches, the production of which humanity will applaud.

The point which seems most proper for an agricultural establishment, is Cape Belair, a league and a half to the leward of Goree: its soil is a rich black mould, lying on a bed of Lava, which seems to come from the Mamelles It is there that other large vegetables, besides the Baobabs, begin to be more numerous, and which, farther on, towards Cape Rouge, cover, like a forest, all the shores. The wells of Ben, which supply Goree with water, are but a short distance from it, and the lake of Tinguage, begins in the neighbourhood. This lake, which is formed, in a great measure, by the rain water of the Peninsula, contains a brackish water, which it is easy to render potable; it is inhabited by the Guésiks, or Guia-Sicks of the Yoloffes, or Black Crocodiles of Senegal; but it would be easy to destroy these animals. In September, this lake seems wholly covered with white nymphaea, or water-lilly, and in winter time it is frequented by a multitude of water-fowl, among which, are distinguished by their large size, the great pelican, the fine crested crane, which has received the name of the royal-bird, the gigantic heron, known in Senegambia by the venerable name of Marabou, on account of its bald head, with a few scattered white hairs, its lofty stature, and its dignified gait.

Considered geologically, the Island of Goree is a group of basaltic columns still standing, but a part of which seem to have experienced the action of the same cause of destruction and overthrow, as the columns of the same formation of Cape Verd, because they are inclined and overthrown in the same direction.

Cape Verd is a peninsula about five leagues and a half long; the breadth is extremely variable. At its junction, with the continent, it is about four leagues broad; by the deep recess which the Bay of Daccard forms, it is reduced, near that village, to 600 toises, and becomes broader afterwards. This promontory, which forms the most western part of Africa, is placed, as it were, at the foot of a long hill, which represents the ancient shore of the continent. On the sea-shore, and towards the north-east, there are two hills of unequal height, which serve as a guide to mariners; and which, from the substances collected in their neighbourhood, evidently shew that they are the remains of an ancient volcano. They have received the name of Mamelles. From this place, to the western extremity of the Peninsula, the country rises towards the north-east, and terminates in a sandy beach on the opposite side.

Almost the whole north-side is composed of steep rocks, covered with large masses of oxyd of iron, or with regular columns of basalt which, for the most part, still preserve their vertical position. Their summits, which are sometimes scorified, seem to prove that they have been exposed to a great degree of heat. The soil which covers the plateau, formed by the summit of the Basaltic columns, the sides of which assume towards the Mamelles, the appearance of walls of Trapp, but already, in a great degree, changed into tuf, is arid and covered with briars. The soil of the Mamelles, like almost all that of the middle of the Peninsula, which appears to lie upon argillaccous lava, in a state of decomposition, is much better. There are even to be found, here and there, some spots that are very fertile; this is the arable land of the inhabitants. Towards the south, all resumes more or less, the appearance of a desert; and the sands, though less destitute of vegetable mould, extend from thence to the sea-shore. It is by manuring the land, with the dung of their cattle, that the Negroes raise pretty good crops of sorgho. The population of this peninsula may be estimated at ten thousand souls. It is entirely of the Yoloffe race, and shews much attachment to all the ceremonies of Islamism. The Marabous or Priests, sometimes mounted on the top of the Nests of the Termites, or on the walls surrounding their mosque, call the people several times a-day to prayer.

The social state of this little people, is a kind of republic governed by a senate, which is composed of the chiefs of most of the villages. They have taken from the the Coran the idea of this form of government, as is the case with most of those, established among the nations who follow that law.

At the time of the expedition of the Medusa this senate was composed as follows:

Moctar, supreme chief resident of Daccard.
Diacheten, chief of the village of Sinkieur.
Phall.........................Yokedieff.
Tjallow-Talerfour..............Graff.
Mouim.........................Bott.
Bayémour......................Kayé.
Modiann.......................Ketdym.
Mamcthiar.....................Symbodioun.
Ghameu........................Wockam.

  Diogheul, chief of the village of Gorr.
  Baindonlz .... Yoff.
  Mofall .... Ben.
  Schenegall .... Bambara.

  This tribe was formerly subject to a Negro King in the neighbourhood; but having revolted against him, though very inferior in numbers, it defeated his army a few years ago. The bones of the vanquished, that still lie scattered on the plain, attest the victory. A wall, pierced with loop-holes, which they erected in the narrowest part of the Peninsula, and which the enemy was unable to force, chiefly contributed to their success. The Yolloffes are in general handsome and their facial angle has hardly any thing of the usual deformity of the Negroes. Their common food is cous-cous, with poultry, and above all fish; their drink is brackish water, mixed with milk and sometimes with palm wine. The poor go on foot, the rich on horseback, and some ride upon bulls, which are always very docile, for the Negroes are eminently distinguished by their good treatment of all animals. Their wealth consists in land and cattle; their dwellings are generally of reeds, their beds are mats made of *Asouman* (maranta juncea) and leopards' skins; and their cloathing broad pieces of cotton. The women take care of the children, pound the millet, and prepare the food; the men cultivate the land, go a hunting and fishing, weave the stuff for their clothes, and gather in the wax.

  Revenge and idleness seem to be the only vices of these people; their virtues are charity, hospitality, sobriety, and love of their children. The young women are licentious, but the married women are generally chaste and attached to their husbands. Their diseases among the children, are worms, and umbilical hernia; among the old people, and particularly those who have travelled much, blindness and opthalamia; and among the adult, affections of the heart, obstructions, sometimes leprosy, and rarely elephantiasis. Among the whole population of the Peninsula, there is only one person with a hunch back, and two or three who are lame. During the day they work or rest; but the night is reserved for dancing and conversation. As soon as the sun has set, the tambourine is heard, the women sing; the whole population is animated; love and the ball set every body in motion. "*Africa dances all the night*," is an expression which has become proverbial among the Europeans who have travelled there.

There is not an atom of calcareous stone in the whole country: almost all the plants are twisted and thorny. The Monbins are the only species of timber that are met with. The thorny asparagus, A. retrofractus, is found in abundance in the woods; it tears the clothes, and the centaury of Egypt pricks the legs. The most troublesome insects of the neighbourhood are gnats, bugs, and ear-wigs. The monkey, called cynocephalus, plunders the harvests, the vultures attack the sick animals, the striped hyœna and the leopard prowl about the villages during the night; but the cattle are extremely beautiful, and the fish make the sea on this coast boil, and foam by their extraordinary numbers. The hare of the Cape and the gazell are frequently met with. The porcupines, in the moulting season, cast their quills in the fields, and dig themselves holes under the palm trees. The guinea-fowl (Pintada), the turtle-dove, the wood-pigeon are found every where. In winter immense flocks of plovers of various species, are seen on the edges of the marshes, and also great numbers of wild ducks. Other species frequent the reeds, and the surface of the water is covered with geese of different kinds, among which is that whose head bears a fleshy tubercle like that of the cassowary. The fishing nets are made of date leaves; their upper edge is furnished, instead of cork, with pieces of the light wood of the *Asclepias*.—The sails of the canoes are made of cotton.

Several shrubs, and a large number of herbaceous plants of this part of Africa, are found also in the Antilles. But among the indigenous plants, are the Cape Jessamine, the *Amaryllis Rubannée*, the Scarlet Hœmanthus, the Gloriosa Superba, and some extremely beautiful species of *Nerions*. A new species of Calabash, (Crescentia) with pinnated leaves is very common. Travellers appear to have confounded it with the Baobab, on account of the shape of its fruits, the thickness of its trunk, and the way in which its branches grow. Its wood, which is very heavy and of a fallow colour, has the grain and smell of ebony: its Yoloffe name is Bonda, the English have cut down and exported the greatest part of it.

In short, Africa, such as we have seen it either on the banks of the Senegal or the Peninsula of Cape Verd, is a new country, which promises to the naturalist an ample harvest of discoveries, and to the philosophical observer of mankind, a vast field for research and observation. May the detestable commerce in human flesh, which the Negroes abhor, and the Moors desire, cease to pollute these shores! It is the only means which the Europeans have left to become acquainted with the interior of this vast continent, and to make this great portion of the family of mankind, by which it is inhabited, participate in the benefits of civilization.

THE END.

www.ingramcontent.com/pod-product-compliance
Lightning Source LLC
Chambersburg PA
CBHW081214170426
43198CB00017B/2612